COME FORTH
—— IN YOUR ——
ROYAL IDENTITY
WHY SETTLE FOR FIG LEAVES?

Other Books by Marva Tyndale

Ready. Set. Not Yet!
Secrets for Teens about Sex

Recover Your Blessing Birthright
Transforming Lives and Culture with the Gift of Words

911HOPE
When Your Youth or Young Adult is in Trouble
(Audio)

Keeping Our Hope Alive
Strategies to Restore Teens and Young Adults

Co-Authored

Kingdom Chaplains Everywhere
Advancing Spiritual Care and Cultural Transformation
Dudley Mayers with Marva Tyndale

Available @
amazon.ca
realidteaching.org
readysetnotyet.com

COME FORTH
IN YOUR
ROYAL IDENTITY

WHY SETTLE FOR FIG LEAVES?

MARVA M. TYNDALE

SUMMERHILL
PUBLISHING

Come Forth in Your Royal Identity
Copyright © 2025 by Marva Tyndale

Published by: Summerhill Publishing
Shelburne, ON Canada

All rights reserved. No part of this publication may be reproduced in any form, or by any means, including photocopying, recording, or any information browsing, storage, or retrieval systems, without express and written permission from the author, except by a reviewer who may quote brief passages or by students, researchers, or scholars who may use few passages for academic and educational purposes.

All Scripture quotations, unless otherwise specified, are from the INTERNATIONAL VERSION®, NIV® Copyright © 1973, 1978, 1984, 2011 by Biblica, Inc.® Used by permission. All rights reserved worldwide.

Scripture quotations marked (AMP) are taken from the Amplified Bible. Copyright © 2015 by The Lockman Foundation, La Habra, CA 90631. All rights reserved.

Scripture quotations marked (AMPC) are taken from the Amplified Bible, Classic Edition. Copyright © 1954, 1958, 1962, 1964, 1965, 1987 by The Lockman Foundation. Used by permission.

Scripture quotations marked (MSG) are taken from The Message. Copyright © by Eugene H. Peterson 1993, 1994, 1995, 1996, 2000, 2001, 2002. Used by permission of NavPress Publishing Group.

Scripture quotations marked (NLT) are taken from the Holy Bible, New Living Translation. Copyright ©1996, 2004, 2007 by Tyndale House Foundation. Used by permission of Tyndale House Publishers, Inc., Carol Stream, Illinois 60188. All rights reserved.

Scripture quotations marked (NKJV) are taken from the Holy Bible, New King James Version. Copyright © 1982 by Thomas Nelson Inc., Publishers. Used by permission. All rights reserved.

Scripture quotations marked (TPT) are taken from The Passion Translation*. Copyright © 2017, 2018, by Passion & Fire Ministries, Inc. Used by permission. All rights reserved. ThePassionTranslation.com.

Scripture quotations marked (KJV) are taken from the King James Version, which is in the public domain.

ISBN: 978-0-9953000-6-4

CONTACT
416.277.6891
realidteaching.org

Dedication

Lovingly dedicated as a legacy of
hope and empowerment to the generations.

*Let this be written for a future generation,
that a people not yet created may praise the Lord.*

Psalm 102:18

Contents

Acknowledgments ix
Foreword xi
Preface xiii
Introduction xv

LOCATE YOURSELF
1. It's Never Too Late 23
2. The Original You 31
3. Where Are You? 39
4. Understanding What Happened 49

FIG LEAF IDENTITIES
5. Inherited Identity 65
6. Imposed Identity 75
7. Perceived Identity 83
8. Adopted Identity 91
9. Projected Identity 99
10. Let No One Eat From You Again 105
11. Your Quick Personal Checkup 111

GETTING BACK TO ROYALTY
12. The Ultimate Reset and Exchange 117
13. Will the Royal You Please Come Forth! 129
14. What's Holding You Back? 137
15. The Significance of the Royal You 147

THE ROYAL YOU
16. Royal Sons and Kings 161
17. Servant Leaders 173
18. On Kingdom Assignment 183
19. Becoming Who You Already Are 197
20. Roadmap to Your Royal Identity 211
21. Accept and Celebrate Your Royalty 221

About the Author 231
Endnotes 232

Acknowledgments

I am deeply grateful for heaven's partnership that has guided this work from its inception. For many years the initial manuscript laid dormant, yet my heavenly Father, the Lord Jesus, and the Holy Spirit remained faithful to the original plan. At His appointed time, with the breath of heaven, the book has come forth in resurrection power. May the Lord God Almighty be blessed with a bountiful harvest of men, women, and children arising in their royal identity as spiritual sons and kings in each generation. Let Heaven come to Earth!

Many other divinely ordained partnerships made this book possible. With deep gratitude, I acknowledge the directors, associates, and friends of RIDM (Real Identity Discovery Ministries), pastors, authors, intercessors, my husband, and my biological and spiritual family, who made invaluable contributions. Each of you contributed something unique, whether it was investing your time, wisdom, prayers, finances, or gentle nudges at the right time. Thank you for believing in this work as a divine assignment to create a royal identity legacy, especially for the next generation.

To each one who participated in the RIDM distorted identity seminars during the formative years of the ministry, you're perpetually in my heart. Thank you for coming alongside me in allowing the Lord to form His royal identity message in us. By God's grace, we grew up together. May you enjoy a lavish "firstsfruits" blessing.

Special thanks to Andrea Boweya for sharing her heart as a psychotherapist in the Foreword, echoing the hope and opportunities for restoration this book offers. I'm delighted that Boweya Psychotherapy and Legacy Moment Academy provide a safe, faith-integrated pathway to wholeness for a broad demographic, including equipping leaders in Christian communities and personal counseling for men, women, couples, families, and young people.

My heartfelt gratitude goes to Andrew and Juli-Anne James of Summerhill Publishing for the creative intelligence and stamp of excellence that shape everything they do.

Finally, I am overwhelmed with joy to bring this royal identity message to French readers. Jimmy Kansela's partnership was divinely ordained. His support and steadfastness made the delivery of the French edition possible despite time constraints. Mr. Kansela, your commitment to advancing God's Kingdom among all people groups is of great value.

Foreword

As a Psychotherapist for over 20 years, it's no secret that a lack of true identity has become one of the most crippling, soul-deep struggles for countless individuals. It's a battle that transcends boundaries, leaving scars on every soul it touches. Festering at the core of so many hearts are distorted identities that serve as destructive forces, leading individuals to wrestle with beliefs of inadequacy, not good enough, and unworthiness.

In a rapidly changing world, with the influence of social media and shifting cultural norms, the reality of identity has become increasingly complex. For many, the question of who they are and how they fit in can feel overwhelming. Whether whispered in quiet moments of doubt or more overtly obvious through patterns of life's challenges, the lies of a distorted identity can erode the confidence, faith, hope, and success that God intended.

The intersection of distorted identities and Christianity can be an even more challenging space to navigate, fraught with emotional turmoil, spiritual confusion, and silent psychological distress. The tension between personal identity and Christian teachings, when misunderstood or misapplied, can lead to spiritual exhaustion and emotional pain. As a Psychotherapist with a passion for faith-integrated service, I have seen time and time again that when this message of God's identity becomes entangled with cultural patterns, religious dogmas, or unresolved personal wounds, it serves to sustain a distorted sense of self, disconnected from the foundational truths of the faith.

Unresolved collective, spiritual, or personal experiences of trauma, in its many forms, leave an indelible mark on the psyche. It reaches into life's spiritual, emotional, and relational dimensions, creating a ripple effect that alters our sense of safety, worth, belonging, and, ultimately, our identity. All the while, Christianity in its purest form offers a transformative view of your identity, one rooted in the truth that you were created in the perfect image of God and called to reflect this truth in all of life.

I say this to you with confidence — Doing what it takes to restore your true identity is arguably one of the most important steps you can take. It really is foundational to faith, transformation, and life success.

That's why I am so excited that my good friend, affectionately called "the fast forward of my rewind," has so masterfully outlined a transformational and step-by-step roadmap for you in *Come Forth in Your Royal Identity* to do just that! It's truly an incredible resource that everyone needs. It will no doubt support you to restore the identity you have long lost, longed for, and importantly, the identity seized by life's circumstances and lies. I invite you to fully embrace Reverend Marva Tyndale's expressed expectation: "That the Lord will use this book to empower you, along with present and future generations, to joyfully do what it takes to come forth in their royal identity."

Yes, *It is Possible!* By examining both the spiritual and psychological aspects of your identity with sound Christian principles, this book invites you to reflect on how a healthy understanding of self as royalty, rooted in divine love and grace, can lead to genuine healing and wholeness. It calls you to reimagine what it means to be authentically human in the full revelation of Christian love. It invites you to shift away from a fig leaf identity toward a more liberating understanding that God is calling you, at this moment—to come forth as royal.

Rev. Marva Tyndale, you were so created for this assignment! Thank you for deeply inspiring us through your transformation and this timely call to be royal again!

Andrea Boweya, MA, RP
Boweya Psychotherapy Professional Corporation
legacymoments.ca

Preface

I was the least likely candidate for an identity assignment. Well, so I thought, but God knew differently. Although a late bloomer in the discovery of my royal identity in Christ, I came to realize that God had chosen me for this assignment before I was even conceived in my mother's womb. He had designed and shaped everything about me for this purpose. God had factored in all my life experiences, the good, the bad, and the ugly. I eventually discovered that God is extremely economical and wastes nothing.

You'll read later that it wasn't until age forty that God first got my attention to start aligning me with who He says I am. Consciousness is one thing; formation is another. So, I'm grateful that God didn't wait for my complete formation to engage me in the purpose for which He made me. In God's eyes, the transformation process is already finished in Christ Jesus. God sees me complete in Christ through His redemptive blood.

The seed of this book has been incubating for over twenty-two years, starting with an unpublished manuscript and over five seminars on how to be free from distorted identities. After saying yes to God's timing to publish this book, seeing how much content I had on the subject was sometimes overwhelming. A friend's encouragement put things into perspective: "It's easier to curate than create." First Samuel 10:25a also motivated me: "Then Samuel explained to the people the behavior of royalty, and wrote it in a book and laid it up before the LORD."

Come Forth In Your Royal Identity: Why Settle For Fig Leaves? is my offering of gratitude and hope laid up before the Lord. I am grateful for what He has done for me, in me, and through me. This book is also inspired by hope. I have an expectation—that the Lord will use this book to empower you, along with present and future generations, to joyfully do what it takes to come forth in their royal identity. As you go through the pages, may the eyes of your understanding be enlightened.

If you haven't yet come to faith in Jesus Christ as your Savior-Redeemer, I pray that you'll quickly receive the revelation that your quest and struggle to discover who you are and the reason for your existence ends in Him. Your desire for freedom from all that has held you back is satisfied in Him. It's the secret to your fulfillment!

In His Majesty's Service.

Marva Tyndale
Ontario, Canada

Introduction

Next to a knowledge of God, a knowledge of who you are is by far the most important truth you can possess.

– Neil Anderson

The date for one of my identity seminars was fast approaching, and I seized every opportunity to share the invitation. Those were days before WhatsApp, Facebook, Instagram, and other social media platforms made sharing easy. Word-of-mouth advertising and flyers did the work. So, I was delighted when a pastor invited me to a church banquet and encouraged me to bring flyers to share with the leader.

"Who is this for? Christians?" The leader asked, his darting eyes and smirk betrayed his thoughts. He supplied his own answer before I could get a word in. "Any Christian who needs this is in the wrong church." Whether he was right or wrong, I felt no desire to chime in. I knew it wouldn't have made a difference to him. I stretched out my hand to meet his, retrieving the flyer with a heartfelt "Thank you."

In all honesty, however, I must say that in the moment and for the next few days, I struggled with second-guessing the assignment I was sure the Lord had given me. You'll read in chapter one about the life-transforming encounter in which the Lord had commissioned me as His messenger of hope in the escalating identity crisis plaguing people from all walks of life. Believers in Christ are not immune, although we have become new creations in Christ. Our minds need to be transformed to free us from the propensity for distorted identities inherited from Adam when he and Eve used fig leaves to cover their nakedness (Genesis 3:7).

Adam and Eve attempted to create a substitute for their lost glory by covering themselves with fig leaves. We have all inherited fig leaf identities from them. The choice is ours—settle for these false identities or be restored to our original royal identity.

Regardless of our faith persuasion, to one degree or another, we all need to be transfigured by the glorious truths in Christ. Second Corinthians 3:18 AMPC describes the need and process this way:

> And all of us, as with unveiled face, [because we] continued to behold [in the Word of God] as in a mirror the glory of the Lord, are constantly being transfigured into His very own image in ever increasing splendor and from one degree of glory to another; [for this comes] from the Lord [Who is] the Spirit.

Many believers, myself included, have fed on this promised transformation and numerous "I am in Christ" affirmations for years as a regular diet. Yet, the fruit of our diligence has left much to be desired. By God's grace, I understood that something was amiss. We've been trying to become before first unbecoming. (No judgment; we're building awareness here). We've been unaware that we first needed to engage in the process of unbecoming. The need to intentionally divest ourselves of the fig leaf identities we once settled for had been veiled.

So the very seminar the leader had deemed unnecessary for believers, *Freedom From Identity Distortions*, provided the awareness and unveiling we needed to come forth in our royal identity. God faithfully allowed each seminar to speak for itself over the years. The results convinced me of the great need among believers of all ages and liberated me from second-guessing my assignment.

The impact stories have been tremendous. For example, one attendee, a ministry leader, shared that although he grew up in the church and had been in leadership roles for many years, he did not understand his kingly identity. He purchased one of the crowns we made available as a reminder of who he is and the legacy he needed to pass on to the next generation. A single young adult woman received the breakthrough she needed with the truths that helped her to identify the fig leaves she had used to cover her brokenness. She committed to raising a royal family when she married and honored her commitment years later, unapologetically tagging her wedding ceremony as a "Royal Wedding." (In no way was this a copycat of British royal weddings. It was authentic!) As a mother, she has passed on the legacy of her royal identity to her two children. They're being raised with a strong sense of who they are in God's eyes. God's grace will make their pathway to "becoming" much easier, hopefully never settling for fig leaves.

Who am I? Why am I here?

Whatever your faith persuasion, if you're reading this book, you're likely someone who has struggled either consciously or subconsciously with these unrelenting questions: Who am I? Why am I here?

Lasting fulfillment and satisfaction depend on us embracing the truth. Interestingly, as important as these questions are to our well-being, they're bigger than us. They're potential eternity connectors. When answered truthfully, they reconnect us with the Eternal God and King, our Father of Creation, and His eternal purposes that underscore our existence. These questions must be answered based on God's truth. Otherwise, they'll invent answers that seem right on the surface.

You won't find secular concepts about identity here in *Come Forth in Your Royal Identity: Why Settle for Fig Leaves?* You'll find an exploration of biblical truths beginning with the creation of the first human beings, Adam and Eve. You'll see how they made a choice that interrupted God's design and plan for the entire human race. Above all, you'll encounter God's redemptive grace and empowering presence to get you back where you belong so the glorious life you were created for can become your reality.

It's also important to note that the royalty in which our identity is rooted comes from Christ. He is the Firstborn Royal Son of God, King of kings and Lord of lords. We're created in Him and by Him, bearing His royal imprint. Secular monarchical rulers give us a reference point, but they're broken, imperfect representations of the divine pattern.

New Dimensions of Glory

I have a few questions for you to ponder.

What comes to mind when you hear the word glory? Usually, it's God's magnificence, splendor, majesty, and awe that's worthy of worship. His manifested presence as well. Or, it may be the physical and verbal responses such as goosebumps, shivers, silence, stillness, tears, laughter, praise, and other utterances that the sense of God's presence produces.

What comes to mind when you hear, speak, or think of Habakkuk 2:14? "For the earth will be filled with the knowledge of the glory of the Lord as the waters cover the sea."

How about Genesis 1:28 NKJV? "Be fruitful and multiply; fill the earth…" Do you see any connection between these two verses? Have you ever thought that you and I may have a whole lot to do with this filling of the earth with the glory of God?

The heavens certainly have a part, as does all of the natural creation. Psalm 19:1 tells us, "The heavens declare the glory of God; the skies proclaim the work of his hands." What about us, the crowning glory of God's creation? We who have been crowned with glory and honor (as Psalm 8:5 affirms), and through Christ's redemption, have had our glorious image restored? Praying in John 17:22, Jesus said, "I have given them the glory that you gave me…"

Unmistakenly, we share dimensions of God's glory. Therefore, aren't you and I meant to be major contributors to filling the earth with God's glory? ("Be fruitful and multiply; fill the earth…") Could it be that we are yet to grasp the fullness of this revelation? We have all seen and experienced different dimensions of God's glory. Still, there are new dimensions yet to come forth. You are a new dimension of God's glory. It's your time to arise and come forth!

Show Me Your Glory

You're being called to come forth in your royal identity because you carry dimensions of God's glory yet to be revealed—uniquely yours to reveal. Moses' cry to God in Exodus 33:18 is being echoed from the Earth concerning you. Show me your glory!

> For [even the whole] creation (all nature) waits expectantly and longs earnestly for God's sons to be made known [waits for the revealing, the disclosing of their sonship]. (Romans 8:19 AMPC)

As you read along, you'll need to remember that the expression "sons of God" isn't gender-based. It defines believers (male and female) who embrace their spiritual identity. Sons of God are the royal offspring of God the Father with a gender-neutral spirit, created in the image of the Firstborn Royal Son, Jesus Christ, and they function as kings to accomplish their dominion assignment.

Proverbs 25:2 says, "It is the glory of God to conceal a matter; to search out a matter is the glory of kings." With everything within me, I desire to discover the fullness of my royal identity and reveal its unique dimensions of glory to the Earth. My utmost desire is that Christ in me, the hope of glory, will be expressed through me to fill the Earth. How about you?

My passion is for the truths of our royal identity in Christ to be known and experienced. Like a diamond, this glorious reality has dimensions we've yet to apprehend. I assure you, it's never too late, so let the journey begin.

Itinerary

This book takes you on a life-transforming journey through captivating stories, profound biblical teaching for fresh insights, engaging questions to ignite a healing pathway, heartfelt prayers, and empowering words of blessing.

To facilitate your reading experience, I've divided the book into four sections: Locate Yourself, Fig Leaf Identities, Getting Back to Royalty, and The Royal You. Chapter One tells my story and then transitions to God's creation blueprint and the divine GPS God used to help Adam locate himself after he and Eve fell for the serpent's (Satan's) deception. The first section wraps up with insightful teaching on the interruption of God's original design. The chapters in the second section examine five types of fig leaf identities and invite you to do a personal checkup. (Again, no judgment; it's for awareness). The remaining two sections focus on the "unbecoming" aspect of your journey, your coming forth, and fittingly ends with celebration. The chapter titled Royal Sons and Kings is the book's summit, so you may wish to read it more than once.

Come Forth in Your Royal Identity. With a title like this, you can tell the entire book is a call to action. So, I encourage you to invest in yourself (release and enhance your royalty) by completing the Reflection and Action exercise after each chapter.

I am delighted to come alongside you on this royal expedition!

SECTION ONE

Locate Yourself

CHAPTER 1

IT'S NEVER TOO LATE

Every once in a while, God grants His people a rare glimpse of their place in the grand scheme of history — a brief moment when they can assess who they are, where they have come from, and where they are going.

— NLT Commentary[1]

Have you ever resigned yourself to accepting something you desperately wanted to change or fix because you thought it was too late or too far gone? You'll know we're not alone if you know the Gospel narrative of Lazarus' resurrection.

Jesus' friend Lazarus had been dead for four days. Mary and Martha were convinced that if Jesus had arrived earlier, their brother, Lazarus, would not have died. So when Jesus eventually got to the tomb and asked for the stone to be taken away from the entrance, Martha blurted out in John 11:39 what most of us would have said: "Lord, by this time there is a stench, for he has been dead four days." In other words, *It's too late! Why bother?* Perhaps the grief of Martha's loss had jaded her heart and capacity to receive a resurrection miracle.

Jesus' response is as relevant for us today as it was then: "Did I not say to you that if you would believe you would see the glory of God?" In other words, *It's never too late!* After affirming His relationship with His Heavenly Father in prayer, the Gospel account says Jesus cried out with a loud voice, "Lazarus, come forth!" (John 11:43b NKJV)

You guessed it! Jesus' command to Lazarus inspired me to choose the title, *Come Forth in Your Royal Identity*. Jesus' indisputable proof that it's never too late has also inspired faith to believe that despite the many identity distortions we've struggled with, we can come forth in our God-given royal identity. My personal story bears witness.

"It's time to see yourself the way you really are." When I heard these words, I was hundreds of miles away from home at a Women's Conference in Atlanta, Georgia. The speaker, Pastor Laura Pickett, engaged my entire being with her animated style, passion, and enthusiasm. Instantly, I knew I was in for a divine encounter. Through laughter, tears, outbursts of praise, and moments of silent contemplation, I dared to believe it was not too late for me. Despite all the delays and setbacks, God had brought me to the threshold of a brand-new era. In my spirit, I heard and saw what was happening in the unseen realm. I heard the crescendo of a rhythmic sound. The lights dimmed, and the curtains opened. Then, before the debut of this act, I was interrupted by a mental intermission. My recollection of the divine drama that had begun eight years earlier on my fortieth birthday was as vivid as if it had happened only yesterday.

Unveiled Face In A Mirror

Surreal. I had heard people talk about having out-of-body experiences. I was experiencing my first. It was a cold winter morning with sub-zero temperatures and howling winds piercing the silence of early dawn. Clad in woolies from top to bottom and half-asleep, I had stumbled into the bathroom, intending to get back to bed as fast as possible. The cozy warmth of my bed awaited me, the perfect place to relish the first quiet hours of my fortieth birthday before anyone else in the household awakened.

Who are you? I stared probingly at the reflection in the full-length bathroom mirror. Pushing past my temporary confusion, I realized I was looking at myself. For the first time! It wasn't the hurried, superficial glances I was accustomed to, not this morning. The image arrested me in unspoken dialogue as thoughts of losing my mind raced in my head. *Who are you?* I pressed harder for an answer, which didn't come, so my musings continued: *I've never seen you before.* Tears rolled uncontrollably from my squinting eye. Unrehearsed words tumbled into the atmosphere. "I'm so sorry… sorry for abandoning you all these years…for not allowing you to see the light of day." Hearing these compassionate words stream from my mouth invited more. "I'm so sorry I've allowed everyone to twist you into a pretzel…I promise to be there for you. You can depend on me."

Although I had no idea what the promise would look like, an unwavering commitment rose within me. More than that, a burning passion to discover the person unveiled in the mirror. Back in bed, I shook my slumbering husband, excited to share the facts; there was no time to tell the story, just the facts—"My life will never be the same after today!" Again, I had no idea what that would look like. All I had was a fierce conviction. For the first time in my adulthood, as far as I could remember, I knew I didn't need someone else's permission to follow my heart.

Eight years later, when Pastor Laura Pickett asked the thousands of women in the auditorium to dig in their purses for a mirror (which she was sure every woman had), there was no mistaking what was happening. God had brought me to the place and time for more unveiling. I was about to get the help I needed to make good on the promise I made to myself. "I promise to be there for you. You can depend on me."

Let There Be Light!

"Look!" Pastor Laura Pickett trumpeted. "You have to see it before you see it!

Like layers of an onion, veils peeled away from my eyes with each resounding word. "You are made in the image and likeness of God! You are the God-kind. You are a speaking spirit." The experience intensified when she asked to turn off the main auditorium lights. In a divinely empowered re-enactment of God's first creation command, she echoed: "Let there be light!" The command reverberated. The anointing, power, and weight of each word pierced my heart. And there was light! Literally and spiritually.

Encountering My Glory

In that supernaturally charged moment, I received my sight. I saw my glory. I saw in myself glimpses of the reflection of the glory of God in whose image I was created! Seeing dimly at first, I felt like the man who said he saw men as trees walking around while Jesus restored his sight.[2] I began seeing myself in a different light! My perception was much clearer than the encounter that started my journey of discovering my real identity eight years earlier on my fortieth birthday.

These verses intensified my vision and glory encounters.

> For now we see in a mirror, dimly, but then face to face. Now I know in part, but then I shall know just as I also am known. (1 Corinthians 13:12 NKJV)

> But we all, with unveiled face, beholding as in a mirror the glory of the Lord, are being transformed into the same image from glory to glory, just as by the Spirit of the Lord. (2 Corinthians 3:18 NKJV)

The translation of the Greek word *doxa* is glory, which we usually relate to our worship of God, His majesty and splendor. However, what's not so well known is that *doxa* also means "opinion, judgment, or view."[3] God had used these divine encounters to radically change my opinion, judgment, and view of myself—forever! Seeing myself from God's vantage point, I began the journey of discovering the unique dimension of His glory He had invested in me.

Why Me? Isn't It Too Late?

Ever so gently and with His all-consuming love, the Lord showed me a vision of millions of people struggling with their identity. Like me, many were in the church, stuck in the same ignorance and confusion He had just rescued me from. *"I'm sending you to them, and you'll also reach children through them."* My mind formulated one question after another. *How can I help anyone? It has taken me this long even to learn the word identity. I'm a late bloomer. Why me? Isn't it too late? Are you sure?*

Jeremiah 1:5 supplied the answer: "Before I formed you in the womb I knew you, before you were born I set you apart; I appointed you as a prophet to the nations." Then the Holy Spirit impressed upon my heart the Father's thoughts and plans. *"You will speak on my behalf, and because of your experiences, you will identify with the needs of others. I will teach you about identity distortions, reveal hidden truths, and make you relatable to others."*

With God's supply of His all-sufficient grace, I consented and started on a fast track. The name of the ministry I would lead seemed logical: Real Identity Discovery Ministries, abbreviated RIDM. It soon became clear, however, that God had inspired the name. I humbly came to that realization when a friend heard me pronounce the acronym RIDM and told me the correct pronunciation is "redeem." (Get ready for a laugh. With my Jamaican background, I had been saying "rydm," which is how we'd pronounce "rhythm" in our dialect). I chuckle even while writing this. How humbling! Oh, so much grace! Thank you, Jesus, for making something out of my simplicity.

Start At The Beginning

Where do I begin? That was my next question. Today, many messages and teachings on the believer's identity in Christ are available online and spoken from the pulpit. But that wasn't the case when the Lord first commissioned me. In those early years, I cut my teeth on books authored by the late Dr. Myles Munroe and Dr. Neil Anderson. However, it was the Holy Spirit who charted my path. He showed me that I had to go back to the creation of humanity in the beginning for God's revelation of our royal identity blueprint. I needed to understand the glory we had, how we lost it, and how we compensated for the loss with fig leaf identities invented by Adam and Eve.

Divine wisdom dictates that we must first deal with who we have become (which is not who we were meant to be) so we can get to who we really are. I know it sounds like a mouthful, but that's our path. We must unbecome so we can become. Unbecoming involves a struggle, just as it does for the chrysalis that has to lay aside its cocoon to become a glorious monarch. We're committed to the process of unbecoming to become. We're grateful for our partnership with God's presence in the process. We have the spiritual force of Christ's righteousness and His resurrection power working in us. Philippians 2:13 AMPC says it well: "[Not in your own strength] for it is God Who is all the while effectually at work in you [energizing and creating in you the power and desire], both to will and to work for His good pleasure and satisfaction and delight." That's really good news!

Your Appointed Time Has Come

Come Forth In Your Royal Identity encapsulates my heavenly Father's transformational work in my life and the redemptive identity mission He has assigned me. It wasn't too late for me, and neither is it too late for you! We're accustomed to personalizing and praying Psalm 102:13 back to the Lord: "You will arise and have compassion on Zion, for it is time to show favor to her; the appointed time has come." Well, the tables are turned! Now is your set time, your appointed time, to arise and come forth in your royal identity.

You may be light years ahead of where I was when I started the journey of discovering my real identity. Or, you may be a late bloomer as I was. Either way, there is plenty to explore, discover, and experience regarding the royal dimension of our identity in Christ. Esther 4:14 has come to sound like a cliché, but it's not. "And who knows but that you have come to your royal position for such a time as this?" It's your time to come forth in your royal identity for the sake of God's Kingdom purposes on Earth. It's time to fill the Earth with your glory! Over twenty-two years have passed since I heard, "It's time to see yourself the way you really are." May these words also change the trajectory of your life as they changed mine. With God, all things are possible!

P.S. If you had skipped the introduction, I encourage you to go back and read it, as it's a good foundation from which to launch.

Reflection and Action

What insights did you gain from this chapter?

_____

_____

_____

_____

Specify at least two actions you'll take based on the insights gained.

1. _____

_____

2. _____

_____

CHAPTER 2

THE ORIGINAL YOU

*If you want to know who you are, look at God.
The key to understanding life is in the source of life, not in the life itself.*

– Dr. Myles Munroe

In many respects, our human existence is a journey back to our royal identity. One of the secrets to making the journey successful (fulfilling) is to start at the beginning, understand God's Genesis creation blueprint, and embrace it. I've had some wise counsel from the Holy Spirit — "Don't take it for granted that people know the truths of their origin or how the choice of the first created humans, Adam and Eve, distorted the human identity." This counsel resonated deeply with me because, for a long time, I only thought of my origin from a biological (parental) perspective.

There's no shortage of opinions about the origin of humanity and what happened to Adam and Eve in the Garden of Eden. Even people who've never read the Bible have ideas. The biblical facts aren't well known, and the mysteries of God's intent are even less known. We'll use this chapter for vital foundation work. You may already know the creation narrative. However, as you read, you'll want to be open to fresh insights.

God's Masterpiece

After five days of speaking creation into existence, God reached the zenith of His creation work. Everything He did up to this point was preparation to bring forth His masterpiece—humanity. You and I are the *magnum opus* of God's creation!

The Psalmist David had this revelation and lavished praise on God. In Psalm 139:14, he says, "I praise you because I am fearfully and wonderfully made; your works are wonderful, I know that full well." The expression of awe in the Passion Translation of this verse is beautiful: "I thank you, God, for making me so mysteriously complex! Everything you do is marvelously breathtaking. It simply amazes me to think about it!"

In Ephesians 2:10, the Apostle Paul affirms the reinstatement of God's original design on the other side of sin's disruption and Christ's redemption. The New Living Translation reads: "For we are God's masterpiece. He has created us anew in Christ Jesus, so we can do the good things he planned for us long ago."

The Creation Blueprint

A pattern emerges from God's creation work. God spoke to the source from which He wanted to produce the creation so that it would share its source's constitution (makeup) and function best when connected to that source. For the creation of the celestial bodies, God spoke to the atmospheric gases (Genesis 1:14). For plants and animals, He spoke to the soil (Genesis 1:11, 24). For marine life, God spoke to the water (Genesis 1:20). For winged creatures, He spoke to the expanse of the sky. But for the creation of humanity, God spoke to Himself!

> Then God said, "Let Us make man in Our image, according to Our likeness; let them have dominion over the fish of the sea, over the birds of the air, and over the cattle, over all the earth and over every creeping thing that creeps on the earth." So God created man in His own image; in the image of God He created him; male and female He created them. (Genesis 1:26-27 NKJV)

These verses establish humanity's source, design, and purpose. The Source is God (the Trinity of Father, Son, and Holy Spirit). The design is a photocopy of God's image and likeness. The purpose is dominion. In other words, we are of the God-kind. John 4:24 tells us God is Spirit.

With God as our Source, first of all it means we're constituted with God's Spirit essence as spirit beings. Secondly, like the rest of creation, we must remain connected to Him as our Source to experience our best life. Thirdly, our existence is purposeful. We're all here on purpose!

For a deeper understanding of the blueprint, we'll examine a few specific dimensions: God's righteousness and glory, the gender-neutral spirit of humanity, the biological male and female, and humanity's three-part design.

God's righteousness and glory

Of the many implications of being created in the image and likeness of God, His righteousness and glory are noteworthy. These dimensions of God's identity in us are not as well known. Neither is the impact that Adam's choice had on them. They're not readily identifiable from the Genesis narrative, but we find specific references elsewhere, such as these:

> The LORD is righteous in all his ways and faithful in all he does. (Psalm 145:17)
>
> God made him who had no sin to be sin for us, so that in him we might become the righteousness of God. (2 Corinthians 5:21)
>
> The LORD wraps himself in light as with a garment. (Psalm 104:2)
>
> What are mere mortals that you should think about them, human beings that you should care for them? Yet you made them only a little lower than God and **crowned them with glory and honor**. You gave them charge of everything you made, putting all things under their authority. (Psalm 8:4-6 NLT, emphasis added)

At creation, God bestowed dimensions of His glory upon us as a covering of light and as a crown of glory and honor. Since we originated from God as our Source, we also share His righteousness (moral perfection, being just and virtuous) as part of our intrinsic nature or constitution. We were created with God's righteousness in our DNA and His glory as our covering. As you will see later, these dimensions of God's identity in us became the prime targets of Satan's deception.

Likewise, they also became prime targets of Jesus' redemptive work to get us back to God's original identity.

> God made him who had no sin to be sin for us, so that in him we might become the righteousness of God. (2 Corinthians 5:21)

> I have given them the glory that you gave me, that they may be one as we are one. (John 17:22)

The gender-neutral spirit of humanity

We understand from the creation narrative that Adam was the first man created by God. What's not always understood, however, is that God first created man as a gender-neutral spirit. The reference to "man" in Genesis 1:26 KJV ("Let us make *man* in our image") does not mean a biological male. In that verse, the Hebrew word for man is a collective term for humanity, *'adam*. Specifically, this term describes the gender-neutral spirit God first called out from Himself in creating humanity. God then placed this "spirit-man" in separate biological male and female bodies, Adam and Eve.

Biological male and female

Genesis 1:27 can be confusing unless we understand that it summarizes the two-step creation process of the gender-neutral spirit of humanity (*'adam*) and gender-specific biological bodies (Adam and Eve) to host the spirit.

> So God created man in his own image, in the image of God created he him; male and female created he them. (KJV)

Elaborating on the creation account, Genesis 2:4-7 records the formation of the male biological body with a soul.

> This is the account of the heavens and the earth when they were created, when the LORD God made the earth and the heavens. Now no shrub had yet appeared on the earth and no plant had yet sprung up, for the LORD God had not sent rain on the earth and there was no one to work the ground, but streams came up from the earth and watered the whole surface of the ground. Then the LORD God formed a man from the dust of the ground and breathed into his nostrils

the breath of life, and the man became a living being.

Genesis 2 later records the first use of the name Adam (ruddy from red soil) for the biological male and the formation of the female, first named Woman, then Eve.

> The LORD God said, "It is not good for the man to be alone. I will make a helper suitable for him." So the LORD God caused the man to fall into a deep sleep; and while he was sleeping, he took one of the man's ribs and then closed up the place with flesh. Then the LORD God made a woman from the rib he had taken out of the man, and he brought her to the man. The man said, "This is now bone of my bones and flesh of my flesh; she shall be called 'woman,' for she was taken out of man." (Genesis 2:18, 21-23)

According to God's creation design, a physical body is necessary to function on Earth. So God gave us male and female physical bodies to host our gender-neutral spirit and to function in the Earth realm.

Spirit, soul, and body

God is an Intelligent Designer and was purposeful in creating humanity as a three-part being: spirit, soul, and body. Genesis 1:27 and Genesis 2:4-7 which you read earlier, give us this blueprint design. In the New Testament, 1 Thessalonians 5:23b confirms it. "May your whole spirit, soul, and body be kept blameless at the coming of our Lord Jesus Christ."

We're spirit beings with a soul in a human body. We're not just human beings trying to have a spiritual experience. We're spirit beings having human experiences. A notable significance of our three-part design is that it allows us to function in both the spiritual and earthly realms. We have bi-locational capacity.

The spirit and soul are the unseen, innermost parts of our being; sometimes mistaken as the same, but they're not. They're different, and they function differently. The spirit bears the imprint of God's spirit nature or essence, giving us the capacity for a perfectly divine bond of unity with God. In union with the Spirit of God, the spirit part of our being is designed to lead the soul and body. In other words, we're designed to be spirit-led.

The soul functions as our thinking and decision-making center through the faculties of mind, emotions, and will. The soul receives impulses from the body, which God created with five physical senses to function in the Earth realm: sight, hearing, smell, taste, and touch. The soul, in turn, influences the response of the body. God also designed the soul to receive divine transmissions from the spirit for expression through the body. The soul is like a broker, serving both the spirit and body. However, because it has the faculty of free will, the soul can choose whether or not to cooperate with God's divine order and purpose for its existence. When we discuss the serpent's deception in the next chapter, you'll see how Adam and Eve exercised their free will against God.

Many have asked why God created us with free will, knowing we could (and would) use it against Him. We need to bear two things in mind. First, we're created to function with the faculty of free will like God. Second, our sincere response to God must be done freely, not forced or programmed.

The spiritual heart

The spiritual heart is another non-physical (invisible) dimension of our being, sometimes considered the same as the soul and spirit. While there's some overlap, they're not identical. Proverbs 4:23 presents the spiritual heart in this light: "Above all else, guard your heart, for everything you do flows from it." In technological language, the spiritual heart is like our computer hard drive or cache. Whatever is programmed or stored in our hearts will express itself.

Words spoken to or by us have a powerful impact on shaping the constitution and orientation of our spiritual heart. Even if the words are untrue, they still leave imprints on our hearts.

Beliefs, feelings, emotions, thoughts, imaginations, and actions originate from the pleasant and unpleasant memories of experiences and words stored in the heart. The spiritual heart can also be thought of as the subconscious mind. The limbic system of the brain, a physiological visible organ, functions like the spiritual heart in its storage of memories.

God's Love-Motivated Purposes

God is love. Scriptures like John 3:16 and 1 John 4:16 assure us unequivocally of this truth. God's endless, pure, giving, unconditional love is the motivating force behind everything He does. Two predominant purposes motivated by love emerge from the creation blueprint we've been discussing: Relationship and dominion. Our design as a spirit, with a soul and spiritual heart, in a body, and our bi-locational capacity align with these divine purposes.

Relationally, God desires to be our heavenly Father, the father of a family of human offspring who bear His image and that of His Firstborn Son, Jesus. You and I are reproduced after the God-kind because He is our Father, and we're His children. Internalizing this truth that God the Creator is our heavenly Father makes us secure in our identity. The Fatherhood of God speaks not only of Source but also of love, relationship, belonging, and security. God is the Eternal King (of an invisible heavenly Kingdom), making us His royal offspring, heirs of His Kingdom, and joint heirs with Jesus.

God's dominion purpose is embedded in His relational purpose. We could think of the Genesis creation as God expanding His heavenly Kingdom into another realm—Earth. Who better to represent God and His governmental rule here on Earth than His human offspring? "Let them have dominion…" (Genesis 1:28) sums up our assignment as God's Kingdom representatives and ambassadors. The Garden of Eden was the prototype. Adam and Eve were not only stewards of God's creation. They had a dominion responsibility to reproduce the Eden prototype throughout the Earth.

Together, these two eternal purposes frame the beautiful picture God has of us in our original creation design. We are God's royal family of human offspring and ambassadors representing His Kingdom. At our spiritual core, we're gender-neutral "sons." In our natural physiology, we operate as biological sons and daughters on Earth.

The nature of sincere love is to protect what it loves. So, although God created humanity with the gift of free will and the power to choose, He established a protective boundary for our goodwill. In the next chapter, we'll see how Satan deceptively tarnished Eve's perception of God and violated this boundary to interrupt God's original design and intent.

Reflection and Action

What insights did you gain from this chapter?

_____

_____

_____

_____

Specify at least two actions you'll take based on the insights gained.

1. _____

_____

2. _____

_____

CHAPTER 3

WHERE ARE YOU?

Getting to our royal identity destination requires that we first locate ourselves in relation to where and who we were in the beginning.

— Marva Tyndale

Did you know that the popular children's game Hide-and-Seek is a version of the first game invented by humans? Here's the proof. In Genesis 3:10 NKJV, we read these words spoken by the first man, Adam: "I heard Your voice in the garden, and I was afraid because I was naked; and I hid myself."

There are two big differences between Adam's edition and the classic children's game. Adam's edition wasn't fun, and it wasn't logical. Adam hid out of fear of the anticipated punishment for eating the fruit of the tree God had forbidden him to eat from. Adam's hiding was also illogical and a huge misconception. It makes no sense to hide from someone who already knows where you are. The truth is that Adam's sense of reasoning had become warped. In his deluded and panic-stricken state, it may not have even dawned on Adam that it's impossible to hide from the Omniscient God who knows everything.

Oh no, Adam. God didn't come looking for you or ask, "Where are you?" because He doesn't know your whereabouts. God loves you and wants you to discover that you've had a huge diversion from His set path. He wants you to realize this detour will take you where you don't want to go. He wants to help you locate yourself as the first step to getting back to where you're supposed to be.

I'm not judging Adam because I've often foolishly tried to play the same game. Whether we like to admit it or not, even as believers, hiding from our heavenly Father tends to be our first response after we've chosen our own way instead of His. I pray that through this book, we'll all come away with a deeper revelation of the heavenly Father's unchanging love for us and His deep desire to draw us closer to Himself, especially when we've missed the mark. No matter what, I'm learning to keep running into, not away from, His loving presence. Hiding need not be an option because of what Jesus has accomplished on our behalf through the blood of His cross.

Love Protects What It Loves

You and I know what it is to resist boundaries, although they're meant to protect us. In love and wisdom, God introduced boundaries into the human experience through the two trees in the center of the Garden of Eden. Understanding this protective boundary as a background to Adam's hiding is important.

> Now the LORD God had planted a garden in the east, in Eden; and there he put the man he had formed. The LORD God made all kinds of trees grow out of the ground—trees that were pleasing to the eye and good for food. In the middle of the garden were the tree of life and the tree of the knowledge of good and evil. The LORD God took the man and put him in the Garden of Eden to work it and take care of it. And the LORD God commanded the man, "You are free to eat from any tree in the garden; but you must not eat from the tree of the knowledge of good and evil, for when you eat from it you will certainly die." (Genesis 2:8-9,15-17)

Why was the Tree of Knowledge and Good and Evil off-limits? Humanity, although created in the image of God, didn't have the infinite knowledge and wisdom needed to make perfect choices between good and evil. The limitation God placed around this tree wasn't because God didn't want Adam and Eve to know about the existence of evil. Rather, He intended for them to draw from Him as their Source of wisdom to know and discern between good and evil. God was guarding them from the experience of evil. We don't always have to experience something to know it. We can learn from the wisdom of others. God knew that experiencing evil would change their spiritual DNA. It would pollute the nature and identity of God in them.

The Hook of Deception

In Genesis 3:5 and Genesis 3:22, both God and Satan speak about humanity becoming like God, knowing good and evil. As far as I'm aware, these are the only places in Scripture where we find them saying the same thing.

> For God knows that when you eat from it your eyes will be opened, and you will be like God, knowing good and evil.
>
> And the LORD God said, "The man has now become like one of us, knowing good and evil…"

The first verse is the reasoning the serpent (Satan's agent) used to tempt Eve to act contrary to God's command. The second is God's purpose for His seemingly harsh action of banishing Adam and Eve from the Garden of Eden. God is explicit about the motive behind His actions. He intends to stop them from eating from the Tree of Life (symbolic of eternal life) in their fallen state so they don't live forever, separated from God.[4] On the surface, God and Satan are saying the same thing, but their motives are different. God's words are a loving safeguard. The serpent's words are a deceptive hook.

Eve was already like God. God had made her in His image and likeness, and desiring to express more of the image and likeness of God is a good thing. But that wasn't the serpent's agenda. As Satan's agent, his temptation was an invitation for Adam and Eve to grasp equality with God. Coveting equality with God was the very thing that caused Satan to fall from his glorious state as an angel of God.[5] Having now witnessed God's magnificent design and plan for humanity, Satan was bent on them sharing his doomed fate. He intended to get back at God by corrupting His prized creation and sabotaging His plans for the Earth.

Independence Preceeded Disobedience

Satan's goal was for Adam and Eve to choose independence from God and have the right and power to make the moral judgments between good and evil on their own. God hadn't given humanity this ability. In His love and wisdom, He knew that it would be detrimental without the omniscience and wisdom only God possessed. Satan, on the other hand, offered this seeming opportunity to be like God in deciding what is good or evil exactly because of the demise he knew it would bring.

We've been taught that the disobedience of Adam and Eve led to the Fall of humanity. However, the choice of independence from God preceded their act of disobedience. Through the serpent, Satan had used the gateway of Eve's natural senses, her free will, and her ability to reason to gain her mental agreement with the lie that God was withholding something valuable from them.

> When the woman saw that the fruit of the tree was good for food and pleasing to the eye, and also desirable for gaining wisdom, she took some and ate it. She also gave some to her husband, who was with her, and he ate it. (Genesis 3:6)

Satan succeeded in getting Adam and Eve to rebel against God's authority and supremacy by choosing moral autonomy over dependency on God as their moral guide.

Sadly, the serpent's deception caused Eve's focus to shift from the privilege she and Adam had of having God as their Father, being His delegated authority on Earth, and enjoying the abundance He had provided for them. Eve ended up coveting the one thing they didn't have at the expense of losing everything God had given them.

In typical form, when Adam and Eve fell for the serpent's deception, they didn't consider the impact of their choice. Just as God had warned in Genesis 2:17, they experienced the consequences. The life-giving, sustaining relationship between their spirit and the Spirit of God was instantly severed. Their newly gained independence and knowledge produced instant spiritual death along with shame and fear.[6]

We don't know how much time elapsed before God made His presence known. He could have confronted Adam and Eve immediately, but He didn't. They had enough time to test their newly gained knowledge by making fig leaf coverings. Genesis 3:7 says, "Then the eyes of both of them were opened, and they realized they were naked; so they sewed fig leaves together and made coverings for themselves." Adam and Eve's condition was in sharp contrast to their state at the beginning, as described in Genesis 2:25, "Adam and his wife were both naked, and they felt no shame." The Hebrew word *Ichabod*, found in 1 Samuel 4:21, describes their fallen condition, "The glory has departed." We'll pick up on this loss of glory in the next chapter.

Questions are God's GPS Prompts

You may have heard individuals cleverly change the GPS acronym for Global Positioning System to God's Positioning System. Well, questions are God's "technology" in operating His GPS. When God asks us questions, it's for our benefit, not His.

When God came on the scene, walking in the Garden as He normally did in the cool of the day to speak with Adam and Eve, He didn't accuse, condemn, or lay guilt on the terrified couple. He graciously navigated the situation with questions. God's four questions (three directed at Adam and one to Eve) were His GPS prompts, skillfully designed for location awareness and course correction. God knew Adam and Eve couldn't help themselves in their fallen state. His strategy was to begin the process of moving them forward from awareness to accountability to acknowledgment. God was intentionally preparing humanity for His redemption, enabling us to eventually choose repentance (returning to God's original plan).

Let's join the conversation between God, Adam, and Eve.

Where are you?

Then the Lord God called to Adam and said to him, "Where are you?" So he said, "I heard Your voice in the garden, and I was afraid because I was naked; and I hid myself." (Genesis 3:9-10 NKJV)

God used this first question to make Adam aware that he was separated from his Source and himself. The question reminds me of the repeated phone notifications we sometimes get while using our GPS for directions: "GPS signal lost." The signal loss can happen because of a low phone battery, weather conditions, or physical obstructions of the satellite connection. Spiritually, all of these causes applied to Adam. In essence, Adam's spirit had lost its GPS signal. He couldn't specify his spiritual grid location, so he explained his response to what had happened—nakedness and fear of God's presence.

Having lost his connection with his Source, Adam had become like a fish out of water. He wasn't made to function in this environment of independence from God. He was rapidly losing spiritual oxygen. The last three words of Adam's response are also significant. "I hid myself." Although "myself" isn't included in some translations, there is some indication here that Adam realized he had lost his true self.

Who told you you were naked?

And He said, "Who told you that you were naked?" (Genesis 3:11a NKJV)

This second question is really about listening to the wrong voice. God's question implied more—"Whose voice have you been listening to other than mine?" God wasn't looking for information. He was prompting Adam to be aware he had set the frequency of his spirit to another channel. At first, I thought it odd that listening to his wife's voice was part of God's explanation for the consequences Adam would endure.[7] I then realized God wasn't saying that Adam shouldn't listen to his wife as a general rule. After all, God had made her as his helper.[8]

God was issuing a red alert to make Adam aware that the voice of his wife that he listened to wasn't her original voice. Eve had been conversing with the serpent (listening to Satan's voice and reasoning). By the time she spoke to Adam and offered him to eat from the forbidden tree, like the serpent, she had also become the voice of Satan.

Our hearing and speaking are integral to our makeup. God is a speaking Spirit, and because we're created in His likeness, we also operate like Him as a speaking spirit. Whatever we hear gets into our spiritual hearts and shapes our beliefs. In turn, we speak out of the abundance of what's in our hearts.[9] God created us to hear His voice and speak what He says to bring Heaven to Earth. Jesus demonstrated this alignment of His hearing and speaking when He affirmed in John 12:49-50, "For I did not speak on my own, but the Father who sent me commanded me to say all that I have spoken...So whatever I say is just what the Father has told me to say." Both Adam and Eve had unwittingly reprogrammed their God-designed hearing and speaking frequencies. Their reprogramming to Satanic frequencies would bring Hell to Earth instead of Heaven to Earth.

Another significant purpose for this second prompt was to help Adam recognize the connection between his and Eve's choice and their nakedness. They had lost their covering of God's righteousness and glory. Their condition was a stark contrast to what Genesis 2:25 said about them in the beginning—"Adam and his wife were both naked, and they felt no shame."

God's righteousness and glory are more than items of clothing. They're part of God's identity in humanity. Now, shame had become attached to humanity's identity instead.

Have you eaten from the tree?

Have you eaten from the tree of which I commanded you that you should not eat?" Then the man said, "The woman whom You gave to be with me, she gave me of the tree, and I ate." (Genesis 3:11b-12 NKJV)

You'll notice that God's third question to Adam follows immediately on the heels of the second. He didn't need to wait for an answer because, as with His other questions, He wasn't looking for information. This third question is God's accountability prompt, but Adam sidesteps the question and plays the blame game instead. Adam wasn't only blaming Eve. He was also indirectly blaming God—You gave me this woman.

It's important to remember that because Adam's spirit had lost its connection to God, it wasn't functioning the way God had designed it to function. Adam's soul, which had just gained autonomy, was now conversing with God, not his spirit. It's no wonder Adam avoided God's question and blamed Eve to protect himself.

What is this you have done?

Then the LORD God said to the woman, "What is this you have done?" The woman said, "The serpent deceived me, and I ate." (Genesis 3:13-14 NKJV)

God addressed His final question to Eve. She had been listening to the conversation between God and Adam and heard God's earlier awareness and acknowledgment prompts. God's question to Eve sounded like a condemning criticism. However, it was loaded with the potential to help her recognize the gravity of her actions. She had recalibrated the trajectory of the entire human race.

What was God saying to her? Eve, I gave you and Adam dominion over all creation, including "every living creature that moves on the ground" (Genesis 1:28b). Yet, you've allowed a serpent to talk you out of your dominion authority. Did you know you've given away everything to him? It was Eve's moment of acknowledgment, but like Adam, she also shifted the blame. Her newly independent soul also opted for self-preservation.

How to Benefit from the Genesis GPS Prompts

There's something for us in each question God asked Adam and Eve. They aren't just historical. They're as relevant today as they were then.

Let's recap: Where are you? Who told you you were naked? Have you eaten from the forbidden tree? What is this you have done? (Please don't go down the rabbit trail trying to determine what they ate from the tree. It's a useless diversion).

Here's the key to benefiting from these powerful GPS prompts. We'll likely avoid them if we think they judge us. We'll miss God's purposes and the intended benefit. We'll benefit most by receiving and responding to them as God's recalibrating instruments. Remember, when God asks us a question, it's for our benefit, not His. Let's be aware that these GPS prompts are God's messengers or instructors to facilitate our discovery and rerouting to arrive at the destination God intended at the beginning — to come forth in our royal identity.

At a Dynamic Dimensions Spiritual Health Retreat a few years ago, I spoke about God's first question to humanity. One of the co-hosts underscored the value of this question to us today. She wisely suggested that we change our greeting to help each other locate ourselves on our identity journey. Instead of "How are you?" we need to ask, "Where are you?" Then, if we aren't where we're meant to be, she encouraged us to be honest with ourselves and courageously ask, "How did I get here?"

Redemptive Hope and Grace

After God laid out the consequences of Adam and Eve's actions, He lovingly exchanged their fig leaf coverings for animal skin clothing. Genesis 3:21 says, "The Lord God made garments of skin for Adam and his wife and clothed them." Whenever I read this verse, the image of Adam and Eve wearing animal skin garments dripping with blood always comes to mind. I imagine there was no time to dry out the blood from the garments of skin, so I see them drenched in blood. Genesis 3:21 is a powerful foreshadowing of the Passover Lamb, Jesus, who was slain for the sins of humanity once and for all. Gratitude fills my heart for the blood of Jesus, which didn't only cover humanity's sins but removed them all the way back to Adam and restored us to God's original intent.

Here's good news. The blood of Jesus speaks a better word to us, for us, and over us![10] May we cooperate with God's grace as it recalibrates the frequency of our hearing to the voice of the blood of Jesus.

Understanding how Adam and Eve's choice disrupted God's blueprint is important for returning to our royal identity destination. As we survey humanity's losses in the next chapter, let's do so under the canopy of the redemptive hope and grace that Colossians 1:20 TPT provides: "And by the blood of his cross, everything in heaven and earth is brought back to himself— back to its original intent, restored to innocence again!"

Reflection and Action

What insights did you gain from this chapter?

_____

_____

_____

_____

Specify at least two actions you'll take based on the insights gained.

1. _____

_____

2. _____

_____

CHAPTER 4

UNDERSTANDING WHAT HAPPENED

*But many were amazed when they saw him.
His face was so disfigured he seemed hardly human,
and from his appearance, one would scarcely know he was a man.*

– Isaiah 52:14 NLT

Humpty Dumpty had a great fall. Do you remember this line from the classic children's nursery rhyme about an egg falling off a wall? Having spent endless hours reading children's stories while raising four children, many of these stories have become points of reference, so please bear with me. This fictional character's experience in the nursery rhyme is the perfect metaphor for what happened to Adam and Eve (and all humanity) after they took the serpent's bait and superimposed their will over God's. "Humpty Dumpty sat on a wall,/Humpty Dumpty had a great fall;/All the king's horses and all the king's men/Couldn't put Humpty together again."[11]

The idiom "smashed to smithereens" also captures the aftermath of the choice Adam and Eve were deceived into thinking would have been beneficial. But we know the end of the story. Jesus sacrificed His life to put Humpty (us) together again!

Right here is a good place to interject thanksgiving for the full redemption and reset we can experience through the cross and blood of Jesus Christ. In Christ, we have the divine opportunity to become a brand new creation.

God's glory and righteous identity have been restored to us.[12] I've made known the end at the beginning so you can hold to God's redemptive grace and mercy as you read this chapter and the next section.

Growing up in the church, I often heard about the "Fall" of humanity. I learned that the sin of Adam and Eve's disobedience to God's instruction resulted in instant spiritual death (separation from God). I also learned this powerful truth that John 3:16 was the ultimate restoration remedy. The love of God the Father for humanity was so great that He gave the life of His only begotten Son, Jesus, for our redemption.

In a Good Friday service at the age of fourteen, I heard that God loves me personally and had me in mind when He sacrificed His Son for humanity's sins. This revelation of God's redemptive love captivated my heart. Gratitude and love filled my heart for Jesus as my Savior, and I gladly received Him that day as the Father's love gift to me.

Over the years of leaning into the call of God on my life as an identity messenger of hope, I started to see other dimensions of our identity that were affected by the Fall. The Holy Spirit used many Bible verses and passages to supply missing pieces of the puzzle and connect the dots. This chapter aims to explore the impact of the Fall on our identity that isn't so well known.

First, let me share a powerful identity perspective from the key Scripture for this chapter.

An Identity Perspective from Isaiah 52:14

Not too long ago, a friend sent me the link to a YouTube video from Pastor Dan Mohler titled, *Why was Jesus beaten beyond description?*[13] Pastor Dan explained it this way. "When sin got done with man in the Garden, he didn't look anything like he was created to be. He totally lost His appearance, and you couldn't recognize Him. So Jesus came and got beaten unrecognizable to pay the price for us to get our identity back and the Holy Spirit back on the inside so we can shine."

In securing the full redemption of humanity, Jesus had to become like us. He became sin for us, marred beyond recognition, just as sin had done to us so that we could again receive God's righteousness. In other words, Jesus did it all to put us in the right standing with God and restore us to our original royal identity.

The Interruption of Our Royal Identity Blueprint

The Heart of a Good Thing, written by my dear friend Andrea Boweya, founder of Boweya Psychotherapy and Legacy Moments Academy, gave me new language to describe the Fall of humanity. She introduced "The Interruption" as a concept that captures the effect of Adam and Eve's choice on God's original intent. The emphasis of *The Heart of a Good Thing* is on relationships and inner healing.[14]

Here in this chapter, we'll explore five areas in which the interruption of the Fall directly impacted our royal identity blueprint.

1. Relationship bonds broken.
2. Fatherhood of God rejected.
3. God's righteousness and glory exchanged.
4. Kingdom mutiny.
5. Soul power takeover.

Although the Genesis narrative is our base reference in reviewing these areas of interruption, we'll rely on other Scriptures for a fuller revelation. Jesus' earthly mission of seeking and saving what was lost,[15] His teachings, proclamations, and redemptive work provide a window for deeper understanding. So, in our review, we'll use New Testament revelations to supplement the Genesis narrative. Also, since whatever Adam and Eve experienced applies to all humanity, we'll interchange their names and the word humanity.

Let's prepare our spirit for fresh revelation-insight and a deeper understanding of what happened to humanity in the Fall of Adam and Eve.

Relationship Bonds Broken

God designed relationships as humanity's prime currency. Just as financial currency benefits us materially, relational currency enables us to grow and flourish in all aspects of life. The Eternal God functions in a union of endless love as Father, Son, and Holy Spirit. By creating us in His image and likeness, God planted the capacity for loving relationships with God, others, and ourselves deep within the human DNA.

Maintaining healthy relational bonds is essential for the optimal experience of our true identity, fulfilling our God-ordained purpose, and our overall well-being.

Knowing how vital these relational bonds are, Satan interrupted them at all three levels.

- *At the first level, Adam and Eve lost their spiritual union with God.* God's word of Genesis 2:17 was instantly fulfilled when they ate from the forbidden tree. ("But you must not eat from the tree of the knowledge of good and evil, for when you eat from it you will certainly die.") Adam and Eve's relational bond with God was broken, and they experienced instant death in their spirit. As James 2:26 says, "The body without the spirit is dead." This spiritual death eventually produced death in the physical and other dimensions of human existence. The creation principle of sustaining a vital union with the source for optimal living was interrupted.

  Humanity became like a fish out of water. One of my childhood memories is going to the seaside with my parents to buy fish right off the fisherman's boat. The flailing of the fish in the nets, on shore, and in the boat evoked compassion. Years later, I realized that what I saw was a picture of human existence apart from God. We can no more live separated from God than a fish can live out of water. As the fish needs to be in the water to get its oxygen, we must also remain in union with God for our spiritual oxygen.

- *Secondly, Adam and Eve's relationship with each other was damaged.* The relationship of mutual love, trust, protection, and support that God designed them to enjoy was interrupted. You'll recall from one of the questions God asked Adam that instead of accepting accountability for eating from the tree, he shifted the blame to his wife and indirectly to God. "The woman you put here with me—she gave me some fruit from the tree, and I ate it" (Genesis 3:12). Whenever I read these words, my thoughts often go to Genesis 3:6b, "She also gave some to her husband, who was with her, and he ate it." Adam was right there and could have refused. In today's language, we'd say that Adam threw Eve under the bus. Eve also didn't accept accountability. She shifted the blame to the serpent.

  With this blame-shifting and lack of accountability, the relational union in this first marriage was broken. The brokenness eventually spread to all human relationships, resulting in what Andrea Boweya calls *The Destructive Pattern in Relationship*. "In this pattern, absence, doubt, distorted identity, self-judgment, unfaithfulness, blame, and shame became more evident in their hearts and relationship. They were unwittingly entrapped — They accepted what was abnormal as normal. This separated them from who they were created to be and who they could become."[16]

Pain became a defining factor of the fallen human existence. Not only would the woman experience pain in her childbearing and childrearing, but her relationship and desire towards her husband would also produce pain.[17] The man would experience painful toil in his physical labor.[18]

- *Thirdly, Adam and Eve's relationship with themselves was interrupted.* Being disconnected from God and having come into mental agreement with Satan's lies, their perceptions of themselves became distorted. They had been created to value and love themselves healthily, but they lost the capacity to see the dignity, worth, and love they had in God's eyes. Fear and shame became attached to their self-perception. When Adam said he was afraid because he was naked and hid himself, it was essentially an acknowledgment that he had lost the healthy, loving, relational bond with himself.

  Valuing, honoring, and loving ourselves is highly significant because it affects the quality of our relationships with others. Jesus' explanation of the greatest commandment in Matthew 22:37-40 underscores the significance. "Jesus replied: 'Love the Lord your God with all your heart and with all your soul and with all your mind.' This is the first and greatest commandment. And the second is like it: 'Love your neighbor as yourself.' All the Law and the Prophets hang on these two commandments.'"

In modeling Kingdom values such as love, compassion, honor, loyalty, mercy, and forgiveness, Jesus demonstrated qualities for the healthy relationships we had lost.

Fatherhood of God Rejected

As you read earlier, Adam and Eve's choice to eat from the Tree of Knowledge broke their relationship with God as their Father. The rejection of the Fatherhood of God isn't readily apparent in the Genesis creation narrative. However, from the revelation of God's intent to have a family of human offspring and from what's revealed elsewhere in the Scriptures, we know that Adam and Eve became alienated from God as their Father and Source.

Creation was the work of the Father, Son, and Holy Spirit operating as One. Even naturally, a father represents the source, so we know Father God is humanity's Source. In Luke 3:38, Adam is described as the son of God. When Satan convinced Adam and Eve that God was withholding something and got them to eat from the Tree of Knowledge, he convinced them that God wasn't a good Father. Their disobedience to God's instruction was a declaration of independence from God not only as the Source of their spiritual existence. Relationally, it was a rejection of God's Fatherhood and, indirectly, a rejection of their royal identity as God's offspring.

On the one hand, Adam and Eve's rejection of God's Fatherhood meant spiritual orphanhood, a loss of the sense of belonging and security. On the other, Satan, described in John 8:44 as the father of lies, took the place of God, the Father of Creation. True to his form, Satan flipped Adam and Eve's rejection of God on them and implanted into humanity's fallen DNA the seed of the spirit of rejection.

Revealing God as Father and restoring us to the right relationship with the Father was Jesus' priority in His earthly mission. As Jesus revealed to His disciples in John 14:6-7, "I am the way and the truth and the life. No one comes to the Father except through me. If you really know me, you will know my Father as well. From now on, you do know him and have seen him."

Dying for the sins of humanity and saving us from hell were means to this end of reconciling us to our heavenly Father. Having opened the way back to the Father in the redemptive work of His death, burial, and resurrection, Jesus made it possible to receive the Holy Spirit as the Spirit of Sonship (Adoption), who continually cries Abba Father from within us.[19] In a later chapter, we'll explore how vital returning to the Fatherhood of God is to coming forth in our royal identity.

God's Righteousness and Glory Exchanged

You read in Chapter 2 that we were created with God's righteousness in our DNA and His glory as our covering. These dimensions of God's image and likeness were planted in our constitution and design. They were to be sustained by remaining connected to God as our Source, symbolized by the second tree in the center of the Garden, The Tree of Life. God's instruction to not eat of the Tree of Knowledge of Good and Evil was a protective boundary to safeguard Adam and Eve from receiving into their being a seed that would undermine these inherent dimensions of God's identity in them.

When Adam and Eve ate from the forbidden tree, they lost the gift of being in a right relationship with God and exchanged their righteous constitution for unrighteousness. Influenced by the knowledge gained from the forbidden tree, humanity embarked on redefining righteousness with our self-made standards. We exchanged God's inherent righteous identity for performance or works-based righteousness. This exchange made performance for love, acceptance, and righteousness part of our distorted identity.

Starting with Abram (who later became Abraham, meaning father of nations), God reinforced His universal Fatherhood and reintroduced the standard of faith righteousness. Then, as the Last Adam, Jesus became sin and endured brutal disfigurement on our behalf to reverse what the first Adam did and restore God's gift of righteousness to us.

> And he (Abram) believed the Lord, and he counted it to him as righteousness. (Genesis 15:6. Also Galatians 3:6 and James 2:23)
>
> God made him who had no sin to be sin for us, so that in him we might become the righteousness of God. (2 Corinthians 5:21)
>
> For if, by the trespass of the one man, death reigned through that one man, how much more will those who receive God's abundant provision of grace and of the **gift of righteousness** reign in life through the one man, Jesus Christ! (Romans 5:17, emphasis added)

In Ephesians 4:24, the Apostle Paul encourages us to intentionally lay aside the old self (with its self-righteousness) and embrace our new creation self, which is reconstituted in God's righteousness. "And to put on the new self, created after the likeness of God in true righteousness and holiness."

When Adam and Eve lost God's righteous DNA, they also lost the capacity to bear God's glory image and have His glory covering. As Romans 3:23 says, "For all have sinned and fall short of the glory of God." The glory of God had been Adam and Eve's covering, reflecting their royal identity. Now, with the loss, they had to make their own covering. They exchanged their glory for fig leaf coverings, but God, in His love and mercy, started the process of their redemption through the blood of a slain animal in the Garden. Ultimately, Jesus secured our full redemption through His blood, the restoration of our glory, and set in motion our ongoing transformation.

> And all are justified freely by his grace through the redemption that came by Christ Jesus. God presented Christ as a sacrifice of atonement, through the shedding of his blood — to be received by faith. He did this to demonstrate his righteousness. (Romans 3:24-25a)

> For it was fitting for Him, for whom are all things and by whom are all things, in **bringing many sons to glory**, to make the captain of their salvation perfect through sufferings. (Hebrews 2:10 NKJV, emphasis added)

> But we all, with unveiled face, beholding as in a mirror the glory of the Lord, are being transformed into the same image from glory to glory, just as by the Spirit of the Lord. (2 Corinthians 3:18 NKJV)

Colossians 1:27b fills us with the grace and hope we need to break any agreement we've made with fig leaf identity coverings: Christ in you, the hope of glory. The glory lost has been restored and can now come forth from us to fill the Earth with ever-increasing glory as God intended.

Kingdom Mutiny

From the creation narrative, God gave humanity dominion and authority to rule over His invisible heavenly Kingdom on Earth. In conversing with Eve, the serpent's voice was the voice of insurrection for overthrowing God's plan to establish His Kingdom on Earth through humanity. By getting Adam and Eve to come from under God's authority and declare their independence, Satan usurped their right to rule on the Earth. When Adam and Eve rejected God as Father, they also forfeited their right to the Kingdom as heirs of God and joint heirs with Christ. As described in Second Corinthians 4:4, Satan became the god of this world.

Both Adam and Eve had the authority to rule over the serpent. "Let them have dominion over the fish of the sea, over the birds of the air, and over the cattle, over all the earth and over **every creeping thing that creeps on the earth**." (Genesis 1:26b NKJV, emphasis added) However, neither of them exercised their authority.

Satan doesn't have any new playbook, so knowing full well that Jesus had come to Earth to take back the authority he had usurped, he tried the same strategy with Jesus. Satan's temptations were intended to get Jesus to come from under the authority of His heavenly Father. On the last try, he offered Jesus the kingdom he had illegally obtained.

> Again, the devil took him to a very high mountain and showed him all the kingdoms of the world and their splendor. "All this I will give you," he said, "if you will bow down and worship me." Jesus said to him, "Away from me, Satan! For it is written: 'Worship the Lord your God, and serve him only.'"Then the devil left him, and angels came and attended him. (Matthew 4:8-11)

Jesus overcame as the Last Adam and restored the spiritual authority we lost to Satan. The Luke 10:19 announcement to His disciples also applies to us: "I have given you authority to trample on snakes and scorpions and to overcome all the power of the enemy; nothing will harm you."

Satan's mutiny had also overthrown God's Kingdom rule and authority in the hearts of humanity. So, Jesus was born as a King to restore the invisible Kingdom of Heaven on Earth. He was not setting up a political entity as some thought. He was establishing a spiritual domain, first in the hearts of people. Jesus' Kingdom proclamations during His ministry and His response to Pilate at His trial confirm His intent to restore the Kingdom that humanity had lost.

> The coming of the kingdom of God is not something that can be observed, nor will people say, 'Here it is,' or 'There it is,' because the kingdom of God is in your midst. (Luke 17:20b-21)

> The time has come, he said. The kingdom of God has come near. Repent and believe the good news! (Mark 1:15)

> But seek first his kingdom and his righteousness, and all these things will be given to you as well. (Matthew 6:33)

> Do not be afraid, little flock, for your Father has been pleased to give you the kingdom. (Luke 12:32)

> Jesus said, "My kingdom is not of this world. If it were, my servants would fight to prevent my arrest by the Jewish leaders. But now my kingdom is from another place."

> "You are a king, then!" said Pilate.

> Jesus answered, "You say that I am a king. In fact, the reason I was born and came into the world is to testify to the truth. Everyone on the side of truth listens to me." (John 18:36-37)

By abdicating our God-given authority, we became subject to Satan's dominion (the kingdom of the world). Colossians 1:13-14 NLT tells us, however, that through His work of redemption, Jesus executed a divine reversal and transfer into His Kingdom: "For he has rescued us from the kingdom of darkness and transferred us into the Kingdom of his dear Son, who purchased our freedom and forgave our sins."

As you'll see in the last section of the book, Jesus' restoration of the Kingdom is vital to us being established in our royal identity as kings.

Soul Power Takeover

God designed humanity as a fully integrated three-part being of spirit, soul, and body. We were created to be led by our spirit, with the soul serving both our spirit and body. With the interruption of the union of our spirit with God, the soul gained ascendancy and became the dominant power. The soul was cut off from the wisdom and direction it would have received from the union of our spirit with God's Spirit. The soul was now fueled by independence, impulses of the natural bodily senses, and the influence of ungodly spiritual forces.

Instead of being led by the power of God from our spirit, we became led by soul power. Our spiritual heart was also defiled by the serpent's voice of insurrection and the seed of rebellion received from the Tree of Knowledge of Good and Evil. Self-will, emotional instability, and deceptive thinking became defining markers of human existence.

As the Last Adam, Jesus surrendered His will to the Father to reverse the independence and rebellion that had dominated the human experience through Adam and Eve. He announced in John 6:38, "For I have come down from heaven not to do my will but to do the will of him who sent me." Applying the words of Psalm 40:7 to Jesus, Hebrews 10:7 says: "'Here I am—it is written about me in the scroll— I have come to do your will, my God.'"

Just before His crucifixion in the Garden of Gethsemane, the battle for God's will to prevail was so intense that the Bible says Jesus' sweat became like drops of blood. The ultimate surrender of His will came with this prayer: "My Father, if it is possible, may this cup be taken from me. Yet not as I will, but as you will." (Matthew 26:39)

With the rise of soul power, feelings such as anger, fear, rejection, loneliness, and despair replaced godly emotions such as trust, joy, peace, and hope. Eventually, our own reasoning, logic, and philosophies exalted themselves above God as strongholds (patterns) of the mind.

The soul doesn't surrender its power easily. So, a spiritual battle rages even after we've become new creations in Christ and received new life in our spirit.

> For though we live in the world, we do not wage war as the world does. The weapons we fight with are not the weapons of the world. On the contrary, they have divine power to demolish strongholds. We demolish arguments and every pretension that sets itself up against the knowledge of God, and we take captive every thought to make it obedient to Christ. (2 Corinthians 10:3-5)

Coming forth in our royal identity will require the salvation and transformation of our soul realm so that the life of the spirit, the identity of God in us, and our glory can be expressed more fully.[20]

While our spirit bore the image and likeness of God as the Source of our royal identity, the soul bore the image and likeness of the Tree of Knowledge of Good and Evil, which became the source of distorted identities. To compensate for the interruption of our royal identity and loss of our glory covering, the soul redefined our identity with distorted fig leaf identities.

As new creations in Christ, we've been restored to our royal identity, and that's where our main focus has to be. However, because these distorted identities do not automatically disappear, being aware of them is necessary in the process of unbecoming (transformation) in order to become who we really are. Awareness is key. The cliché, what you don't know won't hurt you, isn't true. The truth is what God says in Hosea 4:6a, "My people are destroyed from lack of knowledge." You'll learn much more about fig leaf identities in the next section.

We've used this first section of the book as the foundation for a better understanding of God's original plan, the interruption of His plan, and the broader implications. We've examined some key areas of interruption: relationship bonds, God's Fatherhood, the exchange of God's righteousness and glory, Satan's Kingdom mutiny, and soul power takeover.

Having gained some understanding to help us locate ourselves concerning the loss of our royal identity, we're ready to transition to the next section. Let's continue building awareness by examining five types of fig leaf identities: inherited, imposed, perceived, adopted, and projected.

Reflection and Action

What insights did you gain from this chapter?

_____

_____

_____

_____

Specify at least two actions you'll take based on the insights gained.

1. _____

_____

2. _____

_____

SECTION TWO

Fig Leaf Identities

CHAPTER 5

INHERITED IDENTITY

From one man he made all the nations, that they should inhabit the whole earth; and he marked out their appointed times in history and the boundaries of their lands.

— Acts 17:26

Based on the creation principle of reproducing in kind, Adam and Eve were empowered to reproduce themselves after the God-kind, the spiritual image and likeness in which they were made. However, they lost that ability when they chose independence from God by eating from the Tree of Knowledge of Good and Evil. Their children and the entire human race would be reproduced according to a warped nature instead of God's original design. Nevertheless, it's important to note that humanity did not cease to be a spiritual being. We retained our non-physical attributes and the capacity to interact with and be impacted by the spiritual realm. Consequently, we inherit more than the physical features of our parents and ancestors.

Human Nature Warped By Iniquity

We've classified our naturally inherited human identity as a fig leaf identity because it emerged from the interruption of God's original royal identity design. To help us understand the distortion, I'd like to say a few things about iniquity, sin, and rebellion. These words are sometimes used interchangeably, but they're different. Also, although we often equate the sin of disobedience with the Fall of humanity, it's important to understand that the warping or distortion of human nature is caused by iniquity.

Author Ana Mendez-Ferrell describes iniquity, rebellion, and sin as the power structure that the devil established in humanity through the seed of the Tree of Knowledge of Good and Evil. With this seed, he contaminated our divine nature in the Fall. She provides this distinction between the three: "Iniquity is the root of evil implanted in man that produces in him the desire to sin. Sin is the fruit that is produced when iniquity is active. Rebellion is the power that feeds iniquity so that it is continually inducing man to sin."[21]

Arthur Burk describes sin as "missing the mark, being out of bounds, over the line, and not measuring up." On the other hand, he says, "Rebellion is quite a bit stronger than sin. It involves willful, knowing defiance of God's rules." He gives this explanation of iniquity: "The root meaning of the Hebrew word translated iniquity is to bend, twist, or warp. When a person seeks to bend, twist, or warp God's absolutes, that is iniquity. Whereas an act of rebellion acknowledges God's rules but defies them, an act of iniquity denies that the absolutes exist or that they apply to the specific situation. Thus, an act of iniquity contests either God's ability or His right to establish absolutes. It represents an attack on the essence of God."[22]

Isaiah 5:20 confirms God's perspective: "Woe to those who call evil good and good evil, who put darkness for light and light for darkness, who put bitter for sweet and sweet for bitter." You'll agree that this is the result of Adam and Eve declaring independence from God to secure the right to decide between good and evil.

When we read about the first families in Genesis, we see the manifestation of many results of the interruption of God's creation design. In Adam and Eve's first generation, sibling rivalry, jealousy, and murder (Cain kills his brother Abel). In Noah's family, we see the dishonor of exposing a father's nakedness in his drunken state. We see Isaac and Rebekah favoring one son over the other and Jacob deceptively taking the blessing his father intended for Esau. Then, more sibling rivalry and jealousy among Jacob's sons led to Joseph being sold into slavery in Egypt.[23] You'll find many other examples throughout the Bible.

Distorted But Useful By God's Mercy

The inherited identity is our default identity as it gets transmitted genetically and culturally. Every human being automatically inherits this distorted identity with distinguishing parental, ancestral, and cultural markers. In addition to being our default identity from birth, three factors, in particular, distinguish the inherited identity from the other distorted identities in their usefulness to God.

First, although the inherited human identity deviates from God's original plan, He still uses the distorted natural reproduction process to accomplish His purposes. The redemptive Seed of humanity, Jesus, would still come through a woman, as God announced in Genesis 3:15 to the serpent (Satan): "And I will put enmity between you and the woman, and between your seed and her Seed; He shall bruise your head, and you shall bruise His heel." God circumvented the defilement of humanity's bloodline by having Jesus conceived in the womb of a virgin by the power of the Holy Spirit, without an earthly father.

Secondly, the inherited identity shows that because of God's mercy, His plans and purposes will not be entirely cut off. Although humanity was not being reproduced after the original creation design, God preserved for Himself people whose hearts aligned with His. The metaphor of Isaiah 65:8 of preserving a cluster of grapes even though much of it is spoiled reflects humanity's inherited identity — "This is what the LORD says: "As when juice is still found in a cluster of grapes and people say, 'Don't destroy it, there is still a blessing in it,' so will I do in behalf of my servants; I will not destroy them all."

Thirdly, throughout the Bible, God demonstrates that families are His priority. He chose the families of Noah and Abram to start over in a new covenant relationship with humanity. In Jeremiah 31:1, the prophet relays God's declaration of Himself as God of all the families of Israel. Also, in Ephesians 3:14-15, the Apostle Paul acknowledges God in prayer as "… the Father, from whom every family in heaven and on earth derives its name."

Despite God's forbearance, we must recognize that our natural inherited identity distorts the royal identity God designed us with at creation. That's why we must apply the blood of Jesus to redeem our family lineage. If we don't and choose instead to define ourselves by our natural inherited identity, it amounts to settling for a fig leaf identity when royalty is our destiny.

Parental Opportunity

By interrupting God's creation design, Satan intended to produce a defiled species of humanity. While Jesus' redemption ultimately reverses Satan's intent, parents have a unique opportunity to partner with God in starting to shape their children's spiritual DNA from the womb. As parents, we're stewards of the children God entrusts to us. When we embrace our royal identity in Christ, we are better prepared to intentionally shape our children's sense of identity according to God's design. Speaking intentional words of blessing over our children from the womb is one of the instruments God gave us as parents to invoke His favor on their identity and destiny.[24]

Dimensions of the Inherited Identity

To understand the natural inherited identity more thoroughly, we'll examine its universal, ancestral, and cultural components. This awareness will empower us to become free of its distortions.

The universal component

When Adam and Eve were cut off from their royal identity, a different nature or disposition was planted in their DNA, becoming the source of the universal inherited identity. Our capacity to function as spirit-led beings was compromised by the soul (mind, emotions, and will) gaining preeminence. Consequently, we've all inherited the identity of a mere physical being dominated by the power of the soul and the senses of the body. Every human being automatically inherits the potential for evil from birth. The Psalmist bemoans this condition over which he had no control and echoes God's lamentation of the human plight.

> Behold, I was shapen in iniquity; and in sin did my mother conceive me. (Psalm 51:5 KJV)

> I have said, Ye are gods; and all of you are children of the most High. But ye shall die like men, and fall like one of the princes. (Psalm 82:6-7 KJV)

With its marred image of God, the inherited identity is characterized by a sense of void, separation, rejection, and insecurity. Intrinsic to this distorted identity is the search for love, acceptance, approval, security, significance, and meaning in life. To one degree or another, depending on our childhood experiences, we have all been affected by these distortions. Only when we embrace our redeemed royal identity as a new creation in

Christ and are restored to the right relationship with God as our heavenly Father are these needs fully met.

The ancestral component

In addition to the universal component that we automatically inherit by being humans, we also inherit the identity unique to the family bloodline or lineage into which we are born. Whether good or evil, these family traits are passed on through the generations because God's design is for His purposes to be accomplished generationally, as Psalm 145:4 reveals: "One generation will commend your works to another; they will tell of your mighty acts."

For example, suppose we were born into a family line of strong followers of Christ. It's very likely, but not a guarantee, that future generations will continue the legacy of faith. Other positive traits of a family line, such as mastery in particular areas of expertise or concentration in certain professions, may also be transmitted. This family pattern usually reflects the "inheritance" God has allotted to that family line to fulfill its particular dominion mandate on Earth.

Inheriting this kind of family lineage is, for the most part, a positive thing. However, it can interfere with our sense of identity when we attempt to answer the life question of "Who am I?" based on our family or ancestral identity. It negates our true Source, God Almighty, our heavenly Father. This natural identity is also subject to change and imperfections, so it's not a secure enough foundation.

Our creation as God's offspring belonging to His royal family is the only secure identity foundation. This awareness is extremely significant for someone who is adopted or in foster care. The sense of identity and belonging they need and deserve will be met when they anchor their lives in the security of their heavenly Father's unconditional love and by acknowledging their identity as His royal offspring.

The inherited family identity portrays strengths and weaknesses, negatives and positives. Someone has said it's a mixture of gold mines and swamps. For most people, however, the negatives outweigh the positives. We all have some degree of negative generational patterns in our family lineages. Often referred to as "generational curses," they're cycles of undesirable experiences and behavior patterns that repeat from generation to generation. Cycles of poverty, depression, suicide, and divorce are examples of distorted inherited identities individuals may use to define themselves unless they recognize them for what they are, reject them, and seek to break off the pattern in their lives.

Here, for example, are some of the distortions by which families may unwittingly define themselves and transmit generational limitations:

"Marriages just don't last in this family."

"We're a poor family."

"Everyone in this family is prone to depression."

"You'll drop out of school just like everybody else in this family."

"There's always so much strife in our family."

Regardless of what we see or experience, this isn't what God thinks about our families. We must recognize that claims like these are nothing more than generational snares. We cannot come to a mental agreement with them.

The cultural component

Like the universal and ancestral components, the cultural component affects us all because we're each born into a social and national community. National or cultural pride has its place in providing us with a certain sense of belonging. As you read in our key verse at the beginning of the chapter, God created the nations and chose where we would be born and live. He never intended, however, for our place of birth or ancestral homeland to be the primary defining factor of our identity. God created us as citizens of His heavenly Kingdom. As Philippians 3:20a says, "Our citizenship is in heaven."

God is our Source, and knowing Him as our heavenly Father gives us the true sense of belonging we desperately need. I have come to acknowledge that while I value my Afro-Jamaican heritage and culture, I can't use it to define who I am. The issue with identities that are strongly based on culture, nationality, race, or even religion is that they distract us from our true Source and our royal identity. Also, they can potentially give rise to racism and atrocities by one people group against another. In cultures where gender discrimination is entrenched, for example, millions of women live and die with the distorted identity transmitted to them and perpetuated by their culture. They have no opportunity to express who God created them to be, to tap into the potential He has invested in them, or the unique mandate God has for them as females.

Where religion plays a dominant role in a particular culture, adherence to that religion can be such a strong defining identity factor that it blocks out the truth entirely. But God did not create us for religion. God created us for a relationship with Himself through His Son, Jesus Christ. Religion is a self-made approach to finding God and meaning in life. We'll never find the true meaning of life, find God, or find our true self through religion, only through a relationship with Christ.

Writing about the new creation life we have in Christ, Colossians 3:11 TPT clearly expresses God's perspective on inherited cultural identities: "In this new creation life, your nationality makes no difference, nor your ethnicity, education, nor economic status— they matter nothing. For it is Christ that means everything as he lives in every one of us!"

Redemption Through The Blood

As you've read, the seed of iniquity established in human nature has distorted our natural inherited identity. When we look at this in the context of the second commandment God gave Moses in Exodus 20:5-6 NKJV, we understand that patterns of iniquity have a generational impact on our inherited identity. "You shall not bow down to them nor serve them. For I, the LORD your God, am a jealous God, visiting the **iniquity** of the fathers upon the children to the third and fourth generations of those who hate Me, but showing mercy to thousands, to those who love Me and keep My commandments." (Emphasis added)

The mercy of God is great indeed! Through faith in Jesus and the power of the blood of His cross, God has made provision for the redemption of our family and generational legacy from negative patterns of iniquity to blessings of mercy for thousands of generations. Becoming born again of the Spirit, as Jesus told Nicodemus,[25] switches us back to God's royal lineage as God intended at the beginning.

Individuals with what may be considered a good family name or background may have difficulty fully embracing their royal identity in Christ even after coming to faith in Christ. However, First Peter 1:18-19 tells us that our natural lineage needs to be redeemed by the blood of Jesus because it has been defiled and has become empty and vain. "For you know that it was not with perishable things such as silver or gold that you were redeemed from the empty way of life handed down to you from your ancestors, but with the precious blood of Christ, a lamb without blemish or defect."

Inheriting God's Righteousness

In the last chapter, you read about Adam and Eve exchanging God's righteousness for unrighteousness. Unrighteousness became part of the human DNA, carrying a consciousness of guilt, condemnation, and shame. The collectivity of sin, rebellion, transgressions, and iniquity is unrighteousness. (Sin includes both the action and the nature).

In His redemption, Jesus took on Himself and became the totality of our unrighteousness (including the sinful nature and lineage), removed it from us, and once again implanted the righteousness of God in our DNA. When the Bible says our inheritance is in Christ, it includes His righteous identity.

> And by the blood of his cross, everything in heaven and earth is brought back to himself— back to its original intent, restored to innocence again! (Colossians 1:20 TPT)

> God made him who had no sin to be sin for us, so that in him we might become the righteousness of God. (2 Corinthians 5:21)

These verses anchor our journey back to royalty, so they'll surface many times.

In conclusion, our natural inherited identity is classified as a fig leaf because it distorts the markers God designed for humanity. Although we tend to define ourselves by our family history, strengths, and weaknesses, God intends that we make Him the Source of our identity. Despite the distortions, God loves our families. Through the blood of Jesus, God has made provision for the redemption of our families back to His original intent. We align with God's desire by choosing not to define ourselves by our family, ancestral, or cultural heritage, whether good or bad. Instead, we must embrace our redemptive lineage through Christ as a new creation.

Reflection and Action

What insights did you gain from this chapter?

_____

_____

_____

_____

Specify at least two actions you'll take based on the insights gained.

1. _____

_____

2. _____

_____

CHAPTER 6

IMPOSED IDENTITY

One isn't born one's self. One is born with a mass of expectations, a mass of other people's ideas – and you have to work through it all.

– Sir. V. S. Naipaul

I recently had a conversation with the father of a teenager who has been gifted with the ideal height for playing basketball. At fifteen, he was only a few inches short of seven feet. Everyone around him, including strangers, said his future lies in becoming a professional basketball player. However, this young man got annoyed when he heard this because he didn't want to be stereotyped. Although he played the game, he wasn't passionate about it. He was responding to another call, the call of purpose, and had already made his career choice. While marching to the beat of his own drum and doing his own dance, others weren't catching on. He was blessed to have a strong enough sense of purpose that insulated him against the identity others tried to impose on him.

We're all vulnerable to imposed identities shaped by the aspirations, expectations, desires, beliefs, experiences, opinions of others, and comparisons. Parents, family, spouses, teachers, friends, others with whom we share community, and even strangers can potentially be a source of imposed identities.

Early Life Stages and Beyond

The formative years, from conception to age six, is the stage at which we're most vulnerable to imposed identities. From a nature versus nurture perspective, we could say that while the inherited identity is nature-derived, imposed identities relate primarily to nurturing. From the words and actions of parents and others, children absorb impressions that they use to define themselves. Having no barometer to evaluate what is false or true, they use these impressions to answer important questions such as, "Am I valued?" "Am I loved?" "Can I trust others?"

Before we proceed, let me assure any parents reading this that I'm not being judgmental. I'm convinced that each of us did the best with the capacity we had at the time. My heart desires to bring awareness to help us identify the source of identity distortion we may struggle with. In addition, I am passionate about helping future generations avoid the mistakes of previous generations. "I missed it, but you don't have to" is the motto that motivates my passion.

When we have little appreciation for God's unique design, purpose, and destiny for each person, we're more likely to fall into the trap of imposing our self-made identity on our children. Imposing an identity on a child may be deliberate or unintentional. Usually, parents mean well, but sometimes, we're motivated by our interests. Typically, it's an attempt to live vicariously through the child to recover a lost opportunity or dream or fulfill unmet needs. We may also be motivated by the desire to preserve a family heritage or the memory of a lost relative.

Inquiring of the Lord concerning a child's purpose and raising the child in the way of that unique purpose will save parents from this pitfall. As Proverbs 22:6 AMPC admonishes, "Train up a child in the way he should go [and in keeping with his individual gift or bent], and when he is old he will not depart from it." As this translation reveals, the intent of this verse goes beyond behavioral discipline.

Another less readily identifiable factor that sometimes influences an identity imposed on a child is the negative feelings or unforgiveness that a parent, especially the mother, may have toward someone. It's now generally accepted that babies in the womb are significantly affected by their mother's physical, emotional, and mental condition. I've known of instances, for example, where the child looks like and eventually becomes like the person toward whom the mother had negative feelings. The condition of the mother's spiritual heart also has a major impact on an unborn child.

Adolescence is another vulnerable stage for imposed identities. At this stage, however, the agents are mostly peers who impose the standard that must be met by those who want to fit in. Identities can also be imposed at other times, such as when we start a new relationship, enter a new community (such as school or church), or begin a new career or profession.

You may be familiar with the subtle or overt pressure people sometimes impose on themselves or others to live up to a particular family identity or standard. In most situations, the person ends up being miserable after pursuing the same profession or line of work as others in the family because it was expected of them. What's sad about these situations is that these individuals lose the opportunity to discover the unique purpose God had ordained for their lives. Although they might seem successful in the eyes of others, they're inwardly unfulfilled. We belong to God first before we belong to our families. God has the right and authority to create each individual for His chosen purposes, even if it's entirely different from what others in the family expect.

The Power of Names and Word

Imposed identities can also be transmitted through the names given to children and the words spoken to them. Names are so powerful in defining identities that a child's name should never be chosen thoughtlessly or carelessly. Names symbolize the person's nature and represent the person's collective attributes, characteristics, and personality. Names also reflect or prophetically announce a person's identity. In the Bible, we see the great significance that God attaches to the various names by which He reveals Himself. God even named children, such as John the Baptist and Jesus, before birth. He sometimes changed people's names to reflect their unique purpose and destiny, as He did when He changed Abram to Abraham, Sara to Sarah, Jacob to Israel, and Simon to Peter.

In John the Baptist's situation, through his naming, the identity imposed on him could have completely altered his destiny. The angel of the Lord had appeared to his father, Zechariah, and told him about the birth of his son and that he should be called John. As a safeguard against Zechariah's negative speaking concerning the miracle of his son's birth, he was struck with dumbness. He didn't speak until the day of the child's circumcision and naming ceremony. Those present wanted to call him Zechariah after his father. However, his mother, Elizabeth, told them he had to be called

John. Zechariah confirmed in writing that the boy's name was John, and at that moment, he regained his speech.[26]

The family and others who wanted to name John after his father expected that he would walk in his father's footsteps as a priest by carrying his father's name. However, the angel's prophecy had announced that John the Baptist's life and destiny were unique. His parents' obedience to God preserved his destiny and identity at the most vulnerable stage of his life. Once Zechariah and Elizabeth had wisely established the foundation for their child's unique identity, it prompted those around to fall in line, although they were puzzled. Luke 1:66 says, "Everyone who heard this wondered about it, asking, "What then is this child going to be?"

The Old Testament has a brief but powerful example of God's grace redeeming someone's name. It's the story of a man whose mother named him Jabez, meaning son of my pain. She gave him this name because of the pain she experienced in bearing him. We're not sure if it was because of the physical pain only or if she had also experienced emotional pain. Still, we can only imagine how devastating it would be to have an identity imposed on us that was defined by pain.

Through Jabez's prayer, God healed his identity, redeemed his name, and blessed him to fulfill his destiny.

> Now Jabez was more honorable than his brothers, and his mother called his name Jabez, saying, "Because I bore him in pain." And Jabez called on the God of Israel saying, "Oh, that You would bless me indeed, and enlarge my territory, that Your hand would be with me, and that You would keep me from evil, that I may not cause pain!" So God granted him what he requested. (1 Chronicles 4:9-10 NKJV)

Verse nine says that Jabez was more honorable than his brothers. Was that before or after God answered his prayer? We don't know. We do know that Jabez could have had an identity of dishonor imposed on him because of the name given to him. There's a similar Old Testament account in the naming of Jacob's last son by his wife, Rachel, who died at childbirth. Genesis 35:18 NLT says, "Rachel was about to die, but with her last breath she named the baby Ben-oni (which means "son of my sorrow"). The baby's father, however, called him Benjamin (which means "son of my right hand")." Thank God for redemption and divine intervention!

Here are a few examples of spoken words that have the power to impose distorted identities upon a person. Since words create worlds, the circumstances and the tone in which words like these are spoken damage our self-perception. They begin to create identity and destiny distortions that God never intended.

You'll be just like your no-good [name of relative].

Why can't you be like _____?

You are never going to amount to anything.

There's redemptive hope! The blood of Jesus is not bound by time and space. It can go back in time and dissolve the impressions that unkind words have left in our souls. God has designed the instrument of spoken blessings to empower us in our identity and destiny. Most of us received disempowering words instead. Well, it's not too late to recover the words of blessing and empowerment God designed you to have at pivotal life stages. A playlist of life-stage blessings on the Real Identity Discovery Ministries YouTube channel will help you do that.[27]

The Church is Not Immune

Believers in Christ can experience imposed identities from the most unexpected source — their faith community. The church can inadvertently become a source of imposing distorted identities on individuals through its codes, standards, behavior, and service expectations. There are some dangers here. To appear spiritual, individuals may prioritize conformity at the expense of their inner transformation. On the other hand, those who don't conform may experience guilt or struggle with feelings of inadequacy or a sense of not belonging. As in families and other communities, the risk of developing performance-based identities increases with conscious or subconscious efforts to be accepted.

While shared values and community norms can help provide structure and guidance, we cannot lose sight of the importance of being real. Alignment with the truth standard of Psalm 51:6 NKJV is a healthy safeguard: "Behold, You desire truth in the inward parts, and in the hidden part you will make me to know wisdom." Also, from Romans 8:29, we know that the image of Christ is our biblical standard of conformity. "For those God foreknew he also predestined to be conformed to the image of his Son, that he might be the firstborn among many brothers and sisters."

A Classic Failed Attempt

In First Samuel 17, we find the classic example of a failed imposed identity attempt. It's the well-known story of the young shepherd boy, David, preparing to face the Philistine giant Goliath in battle. No one in Israel was brave enough to go up against him, not even King Saul. Everyone feared for David's life, and King Saul felt the most he could do was offer David his armor. You're about to read the well-meaning actions of the king to fit David with his battle gear for protection. However, David had a history with God in defeating a bear and a lion and shaping his identity of dependency on God as the source of his victory. David's confidence in who he is and his faith in God gave him the courage to resist the imposed identity that could have cost him his life.

> Then Saul dressed David in his own tunic. He put a coat of armor on him and a bronze helmet on his head. David fastened on his sword over the tunic and tried walking around, because he was not used to them. I cannot go in these; he said to Saul, because I am not used to them." So he took them off. Then he took his staff in his hand, chose five smooth stones from the stream, put them in the pouch of his shepherd's bag and with his sling in his hand, approached the Philistine. (1 Samuel 17:38-40)

The outcome of the battle is phenomenal! David used one of the smooth stones and his sling to kill Goliath. Naturally, we'd think David needed to dress like a warrior to confront a warrior. But would he have killed Goliath wearing Saul's armor? Goliath would have slaughtered him! David's victory was in his own identity as a shepherd boy, simplicity, and faith.

This account is typical of all imposed identities. What others want us to become or do to be like them or someone else just doesn't "fit" us. It doesn't feel right and causes us to feel as if we are living in someone else's skin. Do you remember what it felt like when you were a child and tried walking in adult shoes about three times your size? That's how an imposed identity feels. David's boldness and courage enabled him to fulfill his destiny by refusing to take on King Saul's identity, not only on this occasion but also after he succeeded Saul as the King of Israel. May the Lord grant us the same boldness and courage.

The inherited and imposed identities we've examined so far are from outside sources over which we have no control. However, our response to their influence is what matters in the end. The perceived identity, the subject of the next chapter, is from internal and external sources—how others see us and how we see ourselves.

Reflection and Action

What insights did you gain from this chapter?

_____

_____

_____

_____

Specify at least two actions you'll take based on the insights gained.

1. _____

_____

2. _____

_____

CHAPTER 7

Perceived Identity

But the Lord said to Samuel, "Don't judge by his appearance or height, for I have rejected him. The Lord doesn't see things the way you see them. People judge by outward appearance, but the Lord looks at the heart.

– 1 Samuel 16:7 NLT

People will always form impressions and opinions about us that are different from who we really are or how we want them to see us. Why? We're unique individuals, and our perception of reality is also unique. Rarely do people see us as we truly are. Usually, they see us as they are or from their frame of reference. Whether positive or negative, the perceptions others have of us are almost always distorted. They're not based on the truth of God's Word or how God sees us. Appearance, education, social and economic status, family background, material possessions, religious affiliation, nationality, race, and past experiences are some of the factors others use to form their opinions of us.

In the same way that we don't have to define ourselves based on inherited or imposed identities, we also don't have to be affected by the perceptions others have of us. However, the reality is that even the best of us are sometimes affected. No one is immune. As human beings whose royal identity has been interrupted, we're all susceptible to insecurity. As you'll see, the distorted perceived identity isn't formed only by the perceptions of others but also by how we see ourselves.

The Wemmicks

My favorite children's story is "You Are Special" by Max Lucado.[28] It's about a village of wooden people called Wemmicks. They were the handiwork of a woodworker named Eli, who designed each one uniquely. I think of the story as a modern-day parable with insights into how distorted identities develop from the perceptions of others.

Village life in this community centered around the Wemmicks giving each other gold star or grey dot stickers depending on what they thought of them. Good-looking and talented Wemmicks received gold stars. Undeserving Wemmicks received grey dots. Smooth wood, fine paint, and the ability to perform skillfully earned gold stars. On the other hand, chipped wood and paint, clumsiness, and the inability to speak well warranted grey dots. The system was brutal because more gold stars would be awarded for not having any grey dots. Conversely, more grey dots would be given for not having any gold stars.

Punchinella was one of the wooden village people who received only grey dots. He was distraught because the harder he tried to earn gold stars, the more grey dots he received. Eventually, he met a Wemmick named Lucia with no gold stars or grey dots. He discovered that some Wemmicks tried to give her stars for having no dots while others tried to give her dots for having no stars—neither the star nor the dot stickers stuck to her. Lucia explained that her secret was going to see Eli every day at his workshop and sitting in his presence. By doing this, she knew what Eli thought about her and it made her know that what others thought didn't matter. Lucia encouraged Punchinella to visit Eli, and he did.

Punchinella pushed past his fears and took the trip to Eli's workshop at the top of the hill overlooking the village. Eli had been waiting for Punchinella and extended a warm, loving welcome to him. Punchinella was surprised Eli didn't care about the grey dot stickers that covered his body. Eli assured Punchinella that what the other Wemmiks think of him doesn't matter. All that mattered was what he, Eli, his maker, thought of him. He is special. Of course, Punchinella disagreed and explained why he isn't special, but Eli persisted in affirming why he's special—"You are mine."

Punchinella pondered Eli's words as he left the workshop. "You are special. You are mine." He resolved that what the other Wemmicks thought about him wouldn't matter anymore, only what Eli said. One of the grey sticker dots fell off as he thought about how special Eli said he was. Like Lucia, Punchinella also decided to spend more time with Eli.

It's an amazing story. The Wemmicks mirror our tendencies to evaluate each other and form perceptions that take no account of the unique way God has designed us. We see ourselves in Punchinella sometimes, struggling in one way or another with insecurities and the fear of not being enough for others to celebrate us. Eli's character wonderfully depicts our loving heavenly Father who waits patiently to impart truth to us. We can all take a leaf from Lucia's book. She has the secret. Spending time in the presence of our heavenly Father will reinforce His love for us as the only foundation of our identity. We receive His love as the "bedrock" of our lives.[29]

God Sees Differently

Let's pick up on the title Scripture at the start of the chapter. After Saul had disobeyed God and lost his position as King of Israel, God sent Samuel to Bethlehem to anoint one of Jesse's sons as king to replace Saul. Samuel didn't have any details on which son God had chosen. God said he would show Samuel which one to anoint. Seven sons presented themselves, and upon seeing Eliab, Samuel thought he had to be the chosen one. That's when God gave Samuel His criteria—not outward appearance or height, but the heart condition that only God sees.

God chose none of the seven, and Samuel asked Jesse if these were all his sons. The youngest son, David, was out in the field tending sheep. His father hadn't even included him in the family ceremony. When David arrived, God told Samuel to rise and anoint David because he was the one He had chosen to be king. I can only imagine the shock that went through the family, from father to one son to another. How could David be anointed king? He's a young shepherd boy. He doesn't fit the part!

Sometime later, when Israel looked for someone to face Goliath in battle, his brothers again dismissed David as unqualified to fight. First Samuel 17:28 reveals what Eliab, David's oldest brother, thought about him.

> When Eliab, David's oldest brother, heard him speaking with the men, he burned with anger at him and asked, "Why have you come down here? And with whom did you leave those few sheep in the wilderness? **I know how conceited you are and how wicked your heart is**; you came down only to watch the battle. (emphasis added)

David was not deterred. He went into battle against Goliath, killing him with a slingshot and stone. First, David had to overcome his family's perceptions of him. Then, as you'll recall from the last chapter, he had to resist King Saul's attempt to impose his warrior identity on him.

I think Eliab may have been projecting his heart condition onto David. Eliab's perception of David was the opposite of how God saw him. First Samuel 13:14 and Acts 13:22 give us God's exalted perception of David—a man after His own heart. The question arises in my heart: Whose perception about us will we believe? It's important to note that God's perception of David wasn't because his behavior was perfect. David had a repentant heart whenever he sinned and was committed to doing what God wanted. His leadership as king was submitted to God, the Supreme King.

What Do You See, Parents?

Although not even his family perceived it, David was born with his royal identity— a man after God's heart, the greatest warrior king to shepherd God's people, and progenitor of the natural lineage from which Messiah would come. In the eyes of others, David was only a little shepherd boy whose place was in the field with the sheep, not on a throne or battlefield. The deformed perceptions his family had of him veiled his royal identity. They failed to see the mighty oak in the acorn.

The birth of Moses provides another good example for parents. This example is positive from the start. In Exodus 1:1-22, we read about the prosperity of the Children of Israel in Egypt and the order of the king to kill all boys born to Hebrew women. But the midwives obeyed God and spared many of them. (The King of Egypt was operating as an agent of Satan who wanted to eliminate the seed of the woman destined to defeat him according to God's judgment).[30]

Exodus 2 records the birth of Moses and his mother's actions to save him because, as verse two says, "she saw that he was a fine child." To every mother, their child is "a fine child." Her perception was beyond his physical appearance. By God's revelation, she saw her son's prophetic destiny. By the third chapter of Exodus, we discover that Moses was the deliverer God had birthed to free His people from Egyptian captivity. Had it not been for his mother's ability to perceive a purpose, potential, and destiny beyond her circumstances and what her natural eyes could see, Moses might not have survived.

If you're the parent of a young child, what do you see or perceive when you look at your child? Ask God to give you spiritual vision, eyes of faith beyond what your natural eyes can see. We all need this vision so that when we look at ourselves and others, we see beyond the natural or flawed identity and see the real identity as God sees us. It's time to see ourselves the way we really are from God's perspective.

Lessons From Jesus' Experience

The life of Jesus provides us with many good illustrations of true and false perceived identities. As He performed signs and wonders, the people were amazed at Him, especially those who knew Him to be the son of Joseph and Mary. The religious leaders of the day were particularly confused about the power He demonstrated and the authority with which He spoke. They saw Jesus as a blasphemer and someone who operated by the power of the devil.[31] Others perceived him as demon-possessed and a madman.[32] Many rejected Jesus' real identity for their opinion of who He was.

Some suspected He was the expected Messiah, but many had trouble getting beyond His natural identity as a Galilean and the son of a carpenter. Even Nathaniel, who later became a disciple, was skeptical when Philip told him about Jesus. In John 1:46 he asked, "Can anything good come out of Nazareth?" Nathaniel had formed his opinion about Jesus based on his birthplace and could have missed his destiny as one of the twelve disciples had his perception not shifted.

As the Son of God, with no shadow of doubt about His real identity and purpose, what others thought about Jesus or how they saw Him didn't matter. However, knowing how essential it was for His disciples to have the right perception of Him, He posed some questions to them.

> When Jesus came to the region of Caesarea Philippi, he asked his disciples, "Who do people say the Son of Man is?" They replied, "Some say John the Baptist; others say Elijah; and still others, Jeremiah or one of the prophets." "But what about you?" he asked. "Who do you say I am?" Simon Peter answered, "You are the Messiah, the Son of the living God." (Matthew 16:13-16)

This revelation from God was essential for the disciples to continue Jesus' Kingdom ministry and establish the Church after His resurrection. Similarly, we need a revelation of truth concerning ourselves and others to fulfill God's Kingdom assignment on Earth.

We also learn from Jesus' experience that not even the good perceptions others have of us are a secure enough foundation for our identity definition. People are fickle. They think you're great one minute, and the next, they turn against you. The people who went out to meet Jesus with palm branches and shouted in John 12:13, "Hosanna! Blessed is he who comes in the name of the Lord! Blessed is the King of Israel!" as Jesus entered Jerusalem were the same ones who later cried, *"Crucify Him!"* Only the perception that God, our heavenly Father, has of us is secure enough because He never changes.

Being Our Own Worst Enemy

The experience of the twelve spies God instructed Moses to send to explore the land of Canaan is a classic example of how a self-constructed perceived identity can impact one's destiny. The spies were leaders of the twelve tribes of Israel who had experienced God's miraculous deliverance out of Egypt and through the Red Sea crossing. They had personally experienced God's power, love, and faithfulness. Now, they were being sent on an expedition to scout out the land of Canaan that God had given them as an inheritance. It was a done deal as far as God was concerned.

After forty days, all twelve spies returned, reporting that the land was bountiful, flowing with milk and honey. They even brought samples of the luscious grapes, pomegranates, and figs from the land. They reported that their towns were large and fortified, and giants lived in the land. Two of the spies, Joshua and Caleb, encouraged the community to go up and take the land immediately despite the presence of the giants who were there. The other ten men disagreed and spread this report:

> "We can't attack those people; they are stronger than we are...The land we explored devours those living in it. All the people we saw there are of great size...**We seemed like grasshoppers in our own eyes, and we looked the same to them.**" (Numbers 13:31-33, emphasis added)

What happened? Didn't all twelve men see the same thing? Yes, they did. The difference is that the ten who brought this report (which the Bible called a bad report) had distorted perceptions of the land, the people, and themselves. Their mindset defeated them and cost them their inheritance.

The words God used in judging the behavior of the unbelieving spies alert us to the danger of negative self-perceptions and words. Numbers 14:28 reads, "As surely as I live, declares the LORD, I will do to you the very thing I heard you say." The entire community that sided with the ten spies died in the wilderness, forfeiting the destiny and inheritance God had ordained for them. Although God mercifully spared their children, they suffered the consequences before possessing the land. They wandered in the wilderness for forty years, one year for each of the forty days of exploration.[33]

Based on the examples examined in this chapter, you'll agree that the perceived identity, originating from others or ourselves, is a breeding ground for lost destiny and negative generational consequences. They also promote materialism, envy, covetousness, performance for love and acceptance, and other limitations that hold us back from becoming who God created us to be.

In the next two chapters, we'll look at the distorted identities we're most responsible for: the adopted and projected identity. First, we form these identities by internalizing (adopting) the distortions of inherited, imposed, and perceived identities. Then, from whatever we've internalized, we choose distorted projected identities to externalize.

There's hope. Remember, our goal in this section of the book is awareness. The last two sections are redemptive, highlighting the victories of the blood and cross of Jesus, as well as strategies for experiencing freedom from fig leaf identities so we can come forth in our royal identity.

Reflection and Action

What insights did you gain from this chapter?

_____

_____

_____

_____

Specify at least two actions you'll take based on the insights gained.

1. _____

   _____

2. _____

   _____

CHAPTER 8

ADOPTED IDENTITY

What we believe to be true in our subconscious controls and shapes who we are, whether it is true or not. We are not controlled by truth we are controlled by what we believe to be true.

— Dutch Sheets

The adopted identity is formed by what we believe about ourselves deep in our hearts. It's the conscious and unconscious self-definition based on internalized distortions from inherited, imposed, and perceived identities. Present challenges, our interpretation of past experiences, and their effect on us also contribute to forming an adopted identity. This distorted identity is important to understand because it touches our hearts, beliefs, and self-image. It is also the foundation of the identity we eventually project to others. Since the adopted identity reflects our choice to accept and believe something other than the truth of what God says about us, we must be intentional in not settling for this fig leaf identity. Freedom from adopted identities holds the key to coming forth in our royal identity.

God made us in His image, so the only self-image He expects us to have is the one that reflects Him. On the other hand, Satan's goal is to ensure we never manifest or become who God made us to be. His choice method in reaching this goal is getting us to believe that we aren't who God says we are and cannot accomplish what God says we can do. As you've seen in the earlier chapters, he'll use any source to implant a lie in our hearts and distort our self-image. Still, he cannot succeed unless we take his lies to heart. It's what we believe that ultimately matters.

What We Believe Matters

The ten spies you read about in the last chapter were their own worst enemies. They believed a lie. The problem wasn't in the facts they reported but in their interpretation. It was a fact that the inhabitants were larger in stature, and it was a fact that their cities were well-established. But it was also a fact that God had chosen the Israelites as His treasured possession and had sworn by covenant to give them the land. After being enslaved for over four hundred years in Egypt, they adopted the mentality of slaves, which made them vulnerable to Satan's lies. So, the identity (self-image) they assumed or adopted was that of a grasshopper, believing that the inhabitants of the land also saw them the same way.

Let me say again (it's worth repeating): what we think about ourselves matters! If we don't think about ourselves the way God does, we'll assume a grasshopper identity like the ten spies and not fulfill our destiny. We're who we think we are. By that, I mean we live, act, and operate according to our thoughts and the images that emerge from those thoughts. If our thoughts about ourselves are distorted, our identity will also be distorted. Proverbs 23:7 NKJV says, "For as [a man] thinks in his heart, so is he." Although the context of the verse relates to hospitality, we can apply it to the principle of how our thinking shapes our experiences.

I'm sure you gained much insight from what you read in the last chapter about David and the fictional wooden character Lucia from the Wemmicks village. David and Lucia were alike in that the opinions others had of them didn't matter. Neither of them internalized the opinions and perceptions of others. As a worshipping shepherd, David became the greatest psalmist of all time. Generations after generations have been blessed by his divine revelations and utterances. One could say David grew up in the presence of the Lord. In his relationship with God, he got to know God and himself. Lucia also got to know Eli and what he thought about her by regularly going to his workshop and sitting in his presence for long periods.

As John Calvin, the great Sixteenth-Century theologian and reformer, has said: "There is no deep knowing of God without the deep knowing of self, and no deep knowing of self without the deep knowing of God."

Time spent in God's presence solidified David's self-perception in truth and established him in his royal identity. The same will be true for us.

My Earlier Adopted Identities

From my own experiences, I've realized that Satan doesn't take shots in the dark. He specifically targets the abilities and gifts God has given us to fulfill our purpose and Kingdom mandate. He tries to negate them with his lies.

For most of my life, I believed the lie that I was too shy to speak up about anything moreover speak in public. My upbringing didn't help either because, like most children in Caribbean society, I was raised to believe that children are to be seen and not heard. I was also taught that it was impolite to look an adult directly in the face while speaking to them. When I came to Canada at sixteen, I felt totally inadequate compared to the other students at my school. I struggled with these handicaps up to my thirties.

In the area of my writing ability, the lie was blatant. During my first year in Canada my Grade 12 English teacher told me that I couldn't write or speak English and needed to do classes for English as a Second Language. It meant nothing to him that in my last year of High School in Jamaica, I had passed English Language and Literature in the General Cambridge Examinations administered by his own country (England). I believed him.

However, over the next two years, God strategically used other teachers to start dislodging the lie that had already taken root. The first was my Grade 13 English teacher, who told me after marking my first essay that I had a strong writing ability. I was confused. Then, again, after reading my first essay in university, one of my professors commended me as a gifted writer. Still, it took many years after that to build up the confidence I needed.

Another one of satan's lies that I believed and constantly made excuses about was my lack of creativity. I fully believed and often said I wasn't a creative person. I thought I had lost the opportunity to develop creativity because of the years I had spent working with my dad in business when I should have been doing fun things like other children. Somewhere along the line I had gotten the idea that creativity only has to do with arts and crafts.

Discovering many years later that God had shared His creative attributes with me by creating me in His image and likeness was eye-opening. That was one of the revelations from Pastor Laura Pickett's prophetic announcement that became a defining moment, as you read in the first chapter: "It's time to see yourself the way you really are." I am so grateful for God's redemptive grace and the opportunity to share the gift of my creativity that you're reading right now.

Pressured by Circumstances and Background

The negative circumstances of life have a way of pressuring us to develop limiting beliefs about ourselves. If we're not mindful, our words expose our beliefs and entrench the distorted identity we've formed out of our needs, losses, and unfavorable experiences. God is so faithful that He often challenges the distorted identities we've adopted. He did that for a man named Gideon, who adopted a distorted identity because of the tribe he belonged to and the impoverishment the Midianites inflicted on his people.

We meet Gideon in Judges 6 in a winepress threshing wheat so the Midianites wouldn't raid their produce. An angel of the Lord appeared to Gideon, greeted him as a mighty warrior, and told him the Lord was with him. Gideon didn't feel, think, or look like a warrior, so he objected: "But if the LORD is with us, why has all this happened to us?"[34] When the angel announced that God was sending him to save Israel from the hands of the Midianites, Gideon revealed the wrong belief that had framed his distorted identity. "But Lord," Gideon asked, "how can I save Israel? My clan is the weakest in Manasseh, and I am the least in my family."[35]

Sounds familiar? Our sufferings can cause us to believe that God has abandoned us. Also, by internalizing limiting beliefs about our family background, we can end up adopting a distorted identity. We must guard against comparing ourselves with others because God has a unique purpose for our lives and families. God's unwavering commitment to the purpose He had for Gideon prevailed. He became Israel's fifth Judge and a military strategist who defeated the Midianite army, bringing peace to his people during his lifetime.

Why is the King Hiding Among the Baggage?

You'll find this other Old Testament example intriguing. God had chosen Saul to be the first King of Israel, but something strange happened on the day of his coronation. First Samuel 10:21b-23 NLT reported: "When they looked for him, he had disappeared! So they asked the LORD, "Where is he?" And the LORD replied, "**He is hiding among the baggage.**" So they found him and brought him out, and he stood head and shoulders above anyone else" (emphasis added).

Instead of baggage, some translations say supplies or equipment. Either way, Saul was experiencing great dissonance between God's exaltation of his life and the distorted identity he had adopted. Like Gideon, Saul had a limiting view of himself based on his lineage, and he revealed it earlier when Samuel first told him about God's plan. Saul presented this resume in First Samuel 9:21: "But am I not a Benjamite, from the smallest tribe of Israel, and is not my clan the least of all the clans of the tribe of Benjamin? Why do you say such a thing to me?" In physical stature, Saul towered over others, but on the inside, he was small. Later, in First Samuel 15:17, Samuel reminded Saul that God had exalted him despite his low self-image: "Although you were once small in your own eyes, did you not become the head of the tribes of Israel?"

Saul's kingship highlights valuable lessons as we seek to embrace our royal identity as spiritual kings. Although his reign lasted many years, lingering distorted identities continued to have negative effects on his character, self-image, and relationship with God. He was a jealous and self-serving man. Eventually, his rebellion against God cost him the throne.

Regardless of our past, we have the power of the blood of Jesus to cleanse us of all unrighteousness so we can flourish in our spiritual identity as kings. Before we talk about the snares of social media, the Holy Spirit wants me to release the hope anchor of Hebrews 9:14 NKJV right here. "How much more shall the blood of Christ . . . cleanse your conscience from dead works to serve the living God?"

Social Media Snares

In this digital age, the responsible use of social media generates many benefits for building community, relationships, business, and other areas of life. However, social media can significantly influence the formation of adopted identities, or what we could call copycat or counterfeit identities. Although adolescents are most vulnerable because of the experimentation associated with their life stage, older age groups are not immune. Neither are believers.

It's well-known that most social media postings are curated to reflect a person's best moment or fabricated experience. Rarely do they reflect someone's struggles, true emotions, or the mundane side of life. Nevertheless, these curated images and stories can become a snare to anyone who believes that by adopting the fashion, opinions, or lifestyle of others, they can attain similar popularity or significance.

The psychological damage and spiritual repercussions are serious causes for concern. Adopted identities may produce some rewards, but they're only short-lived. It's impossible to live a lie and be at peace with oneself. Over time, the feelings of inadequacy and insecurity that led to adopting the identity in the first place will only increase.

The Safeguard of Spoken Family Blessings

At the root of adopted identities is a conscious or subconscious dislike of ourselves for any number of reasons. God knew that we needed His blessing on our identity and destiny to have a safe and fulfilling journey through life. Parents are the primary agents He chose to deposit words of love, acceptance, belonging, and significance in our hearts.

When we miss out on the family blessings God intended our parents to speak into our lives at pivotal stages, we become more susceptible to identity distortions than we otherwise would be. However, when we've received our life-stage blessings, they serve as protective walls around us, especially our minds, emotions, and hearts. Like me, you may have missed those words of blessing. There's no need to hold this against our parents. Most likely, they also didn't receive their life blessings.

As you read in the chapter on imposed identity, it's never too late to recover the blessings you missed at pivotal stages of life. My passion is that no one, especially not the unborn and young children, would live without the validation and empowerment that spoken blessings provide. That was the motivation to write *Recover Your Blessing Birthright: Transforming Lives and Culture with the Gift of Words.*

The projected identity is the last of the five distorted identities we're exploring. That's the subject of the next chapter.

Reflection and Action

What insights did you gain from this chapter?

_____

_____

_____

_____

Specify at least two actions you'll take based on the insights gained.

1. _____

_____

2. _____

_____

CHAPTER 9

Projected Identity

*It is not enough for us to be true outwardly – in the self we project to others.
We must be true also on the inside – in the inner parts of our being.*

– Selwyn Hughes

The projected identity represents our conscious effort to hide who we think we are. Projecting our identity of choice gives us the sense of honor, worth, significance, and pride that is otherwise missing. The projected identity is a well-thought-out strategy. Its purpose is to hide our insecurities, fears, and low self-esteem. It emerges as a self-made solution to unmet needs, especially the fear of rejection. As a coping mechanism, the projected identity operates somewhat like a fantasy that enables us to live in a make-believe world. The motive behind the projected identity is to get from others the response, validation, and acceptance we didn't or don't think we'll get by being authentic. It isn't unusual for someone to develop multiple projected identities.

While the projected identity shields us from the fear of shame and rejection, it brings us farther away from our true selves. The projected identity can make us such great imposters and pretenders that others may never know the real person. An even greater danger is that we may never know who we are unless we're healed of this identity distortion.

The hidden message behind the projected identity is that who I think I am is not good enough so this is who I want you to think that I am. I also want you to relate to who I think I am: the pretend me. The late John Joseph Powell, a Jesuit priest and author, gave language to the deep fears that motivate the projected identity: "But if I tell you who I am, you may not like who I am, and who I am is all I have. If I expose my nakedness to you as a person, do not make me feel shame."

The projected identity uses many factors to define itself, such as the trappings of material possessions, the status and prestige derived from work associations and affiliations, a family name, achievements, and titles. Negative factors such as illness, trauma, shame, bad habits, or mistakes can also become a projected identity. But the truth is that we're not our experiences or behaviors. Among believers in the church, compliance with religious standards can also be used to develop a projected identity of being righteous or spiritually mature. Deception and pretense are strongly associated with the charade of a projected identity, so it can become a mental and emotional stronghold depending on the extent to which it has been entrenched.

First-Hand Experience

Long before I knew the word identity or had any clue what a projected identity was, I had one that I valued highly. It was the thing that propelled me to the top as one of three finalists for a very competitive compliance position with a large insurance corporation. With my husband out of a full-time job and me holding only a contract position, this job stood between the family and a financial crisis.

Facing a panel of four executives, it felt like I was in front of a firing squad. It was our third round of interviews and the questions did not get any easier. In wrapping up the interview, the hiring director acknowledged that the decision would be extremely difficult because we were all excellent candidates. But she had one final question: "What sets you apart from the other two candidates?" Without a moment's thought, she had my answer: "I am a perfectionist and will get the job done!"

I left the interview with a job offer! Perfectionism had landed me the job. Little did I know that perfectionism would also have landed me in my doctor's office in less than two years—burnt out physically and mentally. It was time to look inside, and I did. It took many months to identify the source of my perfectionism and bring it into the healing light of Jesus. Like Punchinella, who you read about in the chapter on imposed identity, piece by piece, I gradually let go of my armor of perfectionism. At the same time, I also hung up my superwoman cape.

The Holy Spirit showed me what had happened. I had lost my first love in the pressures of life. I had forgotten the love of my heavenly Father that started me on my faith journey as a teenager. My surrender and return to the healing balm of my heavenly Father's love and acceptance were my paths to wholeness. He eventually transformed the perfectionism and overperformance I had used to define myself into a spirit of excellence that reflected His image in me.

Take Off The Masks

Taking off the masks was a popular sermon subject in the 1970s and 1980s (decades before the Coronavirus pandemic made masks a normal item of attire). While these sermons invited me into authenticity, they left me stranded. I had no idea how I got the masks in the first place, much less how to get rid of them. Struggling with my mental health during part of that season didn't help either. Moreover, it was taboo to seek help for one's mental health outside the church in those days. I am grateful for the healing power of prayer, fasting, and the Word of God. Mustering the courage to receive professional counseling was another lifeline God gave me.

I've come to understand that it's not this or that. We all need permission to heal in whatever way God has made available to us, including the service of psychotherapy. That's one of the gifts this book encourages you to give yourself: permission to get the help you need to heal.

In his book *Why Am I Afraid to Tell You Who I Am?* John Powell lists various kinds of masks people wear. The list is enlightening because it helps us understand that some behaviors and character traits we often take for granted (as just the way a person is) may actually be projected identities.

> The clown, the fragile person, the body beautiful, the all-heart person, the always right person, the people-pleaser, the strong and silent type, the braggart, the competitor, the conformist, the cynic, the dominator, the flirt, the addict, the gossip, the lone ranger, the intellectual, the inflammable, the martyr, the pouter, the worrier, the blamer.

> Each of us wears a mask, a facade we present to the world to protect ourselves from rejection or criticism. These masks are not our true selves, but a strategy to gain acceptance or to hide our vulnerabilities. Whether it is the clown, who jokes to mask pain, or the people pleaser, who sacrifices authenticity for approval, these disguises prevent real connection and understanding.[36]

That last statement is worth repeating: "These disguises prevent real connection and understanding." Projected identities, as a whole, move us farther away from the relational connections God designed us to have with Him and others. We need authentic relationships to flourish, and at no other time in human history have we been deprived of this privilege than in this digital age of social media.

The Big Box Identity Stores

Nowadays, by shopping at big box stores like Walmart and Costco, it's easy to get whatever you want in one place. Online giants like Amazon make it even easier. One-stop shopping is the order of the day. When it comes to identity, the various social media platforms like Instagram, Facebook, TikTok, and Snapchat are equivalent to the big box brick-and-mortar and online stores.

You read in the previous chapter how social media contributes to adopted identities. It's an even more significant breeding ground for projected identities. The adopted and projected identities also reinforce each other. The thoughts and beliefs internalized from following and observing social media influencers are eventually externalized as projected identities. The abundance of trends, ideals, behaviors, beliefs, and lifestyles gives individuals more options than they can handle. So, keeping up can feel like running on a treadmill because of how quickly ideals change and the pressure to conform. The result is that an individual may present multiple projected identities over a short period.

The dangers are real. From God's perspective, it amounts to a form of idolatry—lifting others above God and imitating them. The Apostle Paul admonishes us in Ephesians 5:1 to imitate God as His dear children. And as he says in 1 Corinthians 11:1, we're to imitate him only as he imitates Christ. Secondly, the influencers and those they influence risk being disconnected from the person they truly are. Loneliness, isolation, and lack of genuine connections perpetuate the cycle of distorted identities. Basing our self-worth, value, significance, and sense of belonging on the number of likes and online followers is not only futile. It's a snare. Only the love of our heavenly Father can provide the secure anchor we all need and deserve. Receiving His unconditional love and being intentional about building our real-life relationships are essential.

Fruit of the Tree of Knowledge

Luke 6:43-44 says, "No good tree bears bad fruit, nor does a bad tree bear good fruit. Each tree is recognized by its own fruit." The proliferation of projected identities is a bumper harvest of the Tree of Knowledge of Good and Evil. You'll recall that one of the primary results of eating from this tree is the autonomy to decide for ourselves what is right. In Adam and Eve, we chose independence over dependency on God as our Source. We pushed aside God's absolutes and infinite knowledge for what has been called situational ethics. In our culture today, we're seeing this travesty play out in unprecedented ways.

Nowhere is it more evident than in the area of our personal identity. The Tree of Knowledge has a voice and speaks louder than ever: Define yourself! Choose who you want to be! So, it's not surprising that in today's society, it is acceptable to discard God's binary creation design and choose any preferred alternative. The outcome is an explosion of projected identities. Reflecting on the meaning of iniquity from the chapter on inherited identity, it is not unreasonable to say that some projected identities are a willful warping of God's absolute royal identity design. That may sound intense, so it's okay to take a moment to ponder it. As Maya Angelou once said, "The greatest gift we give to each other is the telling of the truth."

In Colossians 3:9-10 AMPC, the Apostle Paul gives an admonition that we can apply to projected identities: "Do not lie to one another, for you have stripped off the old (unregenerate) self with its evil practices, and have clothed yourselves with the new [spiritual self], which is [ever in the process of being] renewed and remolded into [fuller and more perfect knowledge upon] knowledge after the image (the likeness) of Him Who created it."

I'll close with a fitting question from Pastor Laura Pickett: "If you're busy trying to be someone else, who is going to be you?"

Reflection and Action

What insights did you gain from this chapter?

_____

_____

_____

_____

Specify at least two actions you'll take based on the insights gained.

1. _____

_____

2. _____

_____

CHAPTER 10

LET NO ONE EAT FROM YOU AGAIN

Imagine appearing before the judgment seat of God and discovering, when it is too late, that the real you – the person God intended you to be – never saw the light of day.

– Selwyn Hughes

No! I don't want that for myself or anyone else. It's not just a hypothetical thing. God was intentional in how He created us. Also, in the price He paid to redeem the royal identity we lost. I believe there's an element of accountability here. The question God asked Adam in the Garden of Eden, "Where are you?" is still relevant today and will be at the end of time. I live with eternity in mind, so I greatly appreciate every reminder that this earthly existence isn't all there is to life. We're all in a dress rehearsal for a grand finale.

We've invested five chapters in building awareness about the types of fig leaf identities that plague us (including believers) due to the Fall of humanity. We injected hope along the way, and I trust you've come to this chapter full of expectations. You won't be disappointed.

Jesus' encounter with the fig tree is the highlight of this chapter and section. So, we'll delve into that immediately, then wrap up the chapter with a summary of our findings on the fig leaf identities we've been discussing.

Why Settle for Fig Leaves?

Matthew and Mark's gospel report the fig-tree episode after Jesus' triumphal entry into Jerusalem. We'll read Mark's account because it's more detailed.

> Now the next day, when they had come out from Bethany, He was hungry. And seeing from afar a fig tree having leaves, He went to see if perhaps He would find something on it. When He came to it, He found nothing but leaves, for it was not the season for figs. **In response Jesus said to it, "Let no one eat fruit from you ever again."** And His disciples heard it. . . When evening had come, He went out of the city. Now in the morning, as they passed by, they saw the fig tree dried up from the roots. And Peter, remembering, said to Him, "Rabbi, look! The fig tree which You cursed has withered away." (Mark 11:12-14, 19-21 NKJV, emphasis added)

Interestingly, the King James Version of verse fourteen reads, "And Jesus answered and said unto it." (The NIV you just read says, "In response, Jesus said to it.") There's a dialogue going on here. We sometimes forget that everything has a voice, even if it's not audible.

While we understand that the fig tree in the gospels symbolizes Israel's spiritual barrenness, we have some applications back to Genesis 3 concerning trees and leaves. First, disobeying God's command, Adam and Eve had eaten from the Tree of Knowledge of Good and Evil and plunged humanity into sin. As you know, their action represented independence from God as their Source and the loss of God's righteousness and glory as their covering. Secondly, to compensate for their loss and the resulting nakedness and shame, Genesis 3:7b says, ". . . they sewed fig leaves together and made coverings for themselves."

It isn't coincidental that the fig tree is the only tree in the Bible that Jesus condemned with His words. "Let no one eat fruit from you ever again." Jesus' words concerned much more than hunger and finding no figs to eat. According to the text we read, it was not fig season. Jesus knew that the leaves were a sign that figs would soon appear. He's not unreasonable, so we recognize that something deeper is happening. There's more to the encounter than meets the eye.

Spiritually, the fig tree and its leaves represented the source humanity had switched to when they fell for Satan's deception. Instead of eating from the Tree of Life, they ate from the Tree of Knowledge. It was a source that would offer humanity many empty options that would never satisfy them. Speaking metaphorically in Jeremiah 2:13, the Lord said it like this: "My people have committed two sins: they have forsaken me, the spring of living water, and have dug their own cisterns, broken cisterns that cannot hold water."

Just as the serpent had spoken lies to Eve, the fig leaves that Adam and Eve used as covering also had a voice — the voice of deception. Every fig leaf identity that humanity has formed for itself over time continues to deceive us with lies.

First John 3:8b says, "The reason the Son of God appeared was to destroy the devil's work." If we put this fig tree episode in the context of Jesus' mission to destroy the works of the devil, we'll see its prophetic implications. What Jesus started here with the fig tree, He finished on the cross: He destroyed Satan's works of deception completely. Jesus broke the power that fig leaf identities have over us. We're not victims, and we're not powerless. We triumph in Christ!

You've probably figured it out. These insights into Jesus' encounter with the fig tree inspired the subtitle of the book: Why settle for fig leaves? Jesus didn't settle for fig leaves, and neither should we.

Jesus' response to Peter's observation that the tree had withered has been the subject of many teachings on faith. Let's read those verses because we'll need this God-kind of faith to speak to any fig leaf identities that try to hold us back from coming forth in our royal identity.

> So Jesus answered and said to them, "Have faith in God. For assuredly, I say to you, whoever says to this mountain, 'Be removed and be cast into the sea,' and does not doubt in his heart, but believes that those things he says will be done, he will have whatever he says. Therefore I say to you, whatever things you ask when you pray, believe that you receive them, and you will have them. (Mark 11:22-24 NKJV)

Keep your faith alive, for we'll be moving into faith action in the last two sections of the book. Let's close off this chapter with a quick snapshot and summary.

A Snapshot of Fig leaf Identities

TYPE	ORIGIN	DESCRIPTION
INHERITED	Our natural lineage.	Three components, universal, ancestral, and cultural, all of which bear some mark of the interruption of God's creation design.
IMPOSED	How others expect and desire us to be.	Imposed by others, usually for their own interest and benefit, including parents, teachers, spouses, peers, and others we share community with. Primarily transmitted through nurturing experiences, names, words, and community standards.
PERCEIVED	How others see us and how we see ourselves.	Interpretations, assessments, and opinions based on outward appearance, material possessions, education, family upbringing, and past experiences.
ADOPTED	What we believe to be true about ourselves.	Distorted beliefs (lies) we've accepted and internalized in response to inherited, imposed, and perceived identities.
PROJECTED	How we externalize what we have internalized.	The persona or masks we've consciously or subconsciously constructed from distorted beliefs. They're coping mechanisms that define how we want to be seen and known by others.

Identity distortions are the default identities resulting from humanity's separation from God. Because we lost access to God, the Source of all truth concerning our real identity, we devised our own ways of defining others and ourselves. Satan, a master at counterfeiting, has been all too willing to share his strategies with us in developing counterfeit identities.

Fig leaf identities are artificial, whereas our royal identity is intrinsic. The difference in value is enormous. Being a shoe manufacturer's daughter, I can appreciate the value of quality leather footwear. One of the first things I check out when I look at a pair of shoes is how much of it is fabricated material: the upper, the soles, or both. I expect the price tag to reflect the composition and refuse to pay a high price for something that isn't real leather. Can you see the parallel between real and distorted identities? Why pay a high price for distorted identities that cannot give you the value of your royal identity that you deserve?

Another important characteristic of fig leaf identities is that even if they take little effort to form, they're high maintenance. Ultimately, they all abuse and waste vast resources (time, energy, money) but provide no positive returns. We must be mindful of the need to be intentionally committed to our transformation process so these distorted identities don't linger in the realm of our souls after we've experienced new spiritual birth in Christ. Remember that Jesus has overcome all spiritual forces of darkness that would set themselves against us, and we are overcomers in Him!

The fig tree that Jesus condemned dried up at the root. You can expect the same outcome for any lingering fig-tree identity you need to be freed from. Jesus' words will not return empty. They will accomplish what they are sent to do: "Let no one eat fruit from you ever again."

We're almost ready to launch into section three of the book, Getting Back to Royalty. We'll be activating faith to apprehend all that Jesus has accomplished on our behalf. Get ready for the divine exchange: to trade in the fig leaves for your royal crown of glory, garments of salvation, and robes of righteousness.

First, your Reflection and Action exercise for the chapter, then a Quick Personal Checkup.

Reflection and Action

What insights did you gain from this chapter?

_____

_____

_____

Specify at least two actions you'll take based on the insights gained.

1. _____

   _____

2. _____

   _____

CHAPTER 11

Your Quick Personal Checkup

*To thine own self be true, and it must follow,
as the night the day, thou canst not then be false to any man.*

— William Shakespeare

Congratulations on completing the first two sections of the book! You're halfway through.

Come Forth in your Royal Identity: Why Settle For Fig Leaves? expresses the goal of this journey we've embarked upon together. In aiming for this goal, we highlighted the importance of unbecoming before we can become. So far, we've been focusing on the awareness-building aspect of the process—awareness of creation truths, the interruption of God's creation design, and the resulting distorted identities.

The Tipping Point

The purpose of the exercise in this chapter is to advance from awareness to personal acknowledgment. Acknowledging where you are is the tipping point in freeing yourself from distorted identities. In the words of Pastor Joel Osteen, "Where you are now is not where you will always be. There are brighter days up ahead."

On my part, there's no judgment whatsoever in the exercise. Please join me and be kind to yourself.

Gift Yourself

I invite you to give yourself the gift of a few slow, deep breaths before you begin.

Breathe in for the count of four. Hold for the count of four. Exhale fully.

Repeat a couple of times.

There's freedom in these few intentional breaths. I discovered the power of this gift from the Boweya Psychotherapy Heal Forward Masterclass.

How do these statements resonate with you?

CIRCLE 1-5
(Least to most)

Be in the moment and respond from where you are here and now.

1.	I am growing in my relationship with Jesus.	**1**	**2**	**3**	**4**	**5**
2.	I prioritize meditating on God's Word and sitting in His presence.	**1**	**2**	**3**	**4**	**5**
3.	I believe my heavenly Father's perfect love for me will never change.	**1**	**2**	**3**	**4**	**5**
4.	My heart delights in loving my heavenly Father.	**1**	**2**	**3**	**4**	**5**
5.	Above all, I value who God says I am.	**1**	**2**	**3**	**4**	**5**
6.	Past negative experiences keep popping up.	**1**	**2**	**3**	**4**	**5**
7.	I often find myself trying to please others.	**1**	**2**	**3**	**4**	**5**
8.	I need the recognition of others to feel good about myself and my accomplishments.	**1**	**2**	**3**	**4**	**5**
9.	I compare myself to others and end up feeling inferior.	**1**	**2**	**3**	**4**	**5**
10.	I compare myself to others and end up feeling superior.	**1**	**2**	**3**	**4**	**5**
11.	Keeping up with social trends is a priority.	**1**	**2**	**3**	**4**	**5**
12.	What others say or think about me matters.	**1**	**2**	**3**	**4**	**5**

Gratitude and Acknowledgment

Likely, you aren't where you used to be, yet not where you desire. I invite you to pray with me to acknowledge where you are and embrace gratitude.

Heavenly Father, I am grateful for how far your love and grace have brought me. I surrender this in-between space of unbecoming who I'm not in order to become who you created me to be. I ask you to bless it with grace upon grace.

Thank you for everything you have done through Jesus to bring me back to you. Thank you also for the indwelling presence of your Holy Spirit, who is working in me to finish the good work you have started.

By faith, I celebrate who I am becoming in my royal identity. Amen.

Blessing Your Identity

From the heart of God, your heavenly Father, I bless you with the courage to celebrate your one-of-a-kind royal identity. I bless you with the power to live free from comparison, competition, approval seeking, and confusion about who God made you to be. May you find joy in knowing that in the eyes of your heavenly Father, you're His masterpiece, wonderfully designed to display His glory on Earth. I bless you with great success in becoming uniquely you, the person God had in mind when He created you. And now, may the Lord bless you and protect you. May He smile on you and be gracious to you, show you favor, and give you peace. You are blessed in the Name of the Lord.

SECTION THREE

Getting Back to Royalty

CHAPTER 12

THE ULTIMATE RESET AND EXCHANGE

And by the blood of his cross, everything in heaven and earth is brought back to himself — back to its original intent, restored to innocence again!

— Colossians 1:20 TPT

When Adam and Eve chose their will over the will of God in the Garden of Eden, everything changed for humanity. Merriam-Webster's top definitions of the word everything are (a) all that exists and (b) all that relates to the subject. Romans 3:23 captures the comprehensive, devastating human reality: "For all have sinned and fall short of the glory of God."

On our own, we had absolutely no way to get back where we belonged. With all the wisdom gained from the Tree of Knowledge, we had no way to reconnect with our Source and restore our crowning glory. Humpty Dumpty had a great fall, and there was absolutely no one to put Humpty back together again. But Love came down and did it! Love has a name — Jesus. Jesus did it! Jesus Himself, His cross, and His blood became the Way. Born in human flesh, Jesus came to die a sacrificial death to put everything back in divine order.

Like two sides of the same coin, this chapter is the positive side of the earlier chapter, Understanding What Happened. I'll confess I had moments of distress writing that chapter and had to constantly remind myself of how the story ended. Having this chapter on the ultimate reset and exchange in mind spurred me on. I'm glad we're here! Welcome to the launching pad for coming forth in our royal identity. In the language of author Andrea Boweya (*The Heart of a Good Thing*), this chapter is about "interrupting the interruption."

The Ultimate Reset

John 19:30 records Jesus' final words on the cross: "It is finished!" He had completed the multifaceted redemptive work the Father had sent Him to do. Other than these three words, Colossians 1:20 is the verse of Scripture that encapsulates the totality of God's ultimate reset of humanity's fallen existence. It tells us what He did and how He did it. As you may have already discovered, Colossians 1:20 is the main anchor verse for *Coming Forth in Your Royal Identity*. The Passion Translation is my favorite translation of this verse, followed by the King James Version.

> And by the blood of his cross, everything in heaven and earth is brought back to himself— back to its original intent, restored to innocence again! (Colossians 1:20 TPT)

> And, having made peace through the blood of his cross, by him to reconcile all things unto himself; by him, I say, whether they be things in earth, or things in heaven. (Colossians 1:20 KJV)

Several phrases and words come to life each time I read or meditate on this verse, making it difficult to contain myself: By the blood of his cross. Everything in heaven and Earth. Back to himself. Back to its original intent. Having made peace. Reconcile all things. Restored. Innocence again!

Each expression speaks for itself, but let me comment on the blood of the cross. As far as I'm aware, we find this unique expression only here in Colossians 1:20. We see the merging of the two greatest forces in the universe: the blood and the cross. That's highly significant. The resetting of God's original intent demanded the combination of these two potent forces. We usually think of the physical pieces of wood as the cross. However, from a redemptive perspective, the cross encompasses all of Jesus' work, from Gethsemane to His crucifixion, burial, and resurrection.

Dr. Rajan Thiagarajah explains the significance of the expression "blood of His cross" in this way: "It is only through the blood [that] the power and effectiveness of the cross are revealed. The cross without the blood of Christ has no power or effect on any human being. It is the blood of Christ that reveals the effect and power of the finished work of the cross to every human soul."[37]

It is finished! Our responsibility is to appropriate or apprehend this phenomenal work of redemption and make it our own. The later chapters of the book are designed for this purpose.

The Power of the Blood

In the Garden of Eden, when God covered Adam and Eve with bloody animal skins, He established the requirement that without the shedding of blood, there could be no atonement of sin. Both the Old and New Testaments confirm God's requirement.

> For the life of the body is in its blood. I have given you the blood on the altar to purify you, making you right with the LORD. It is the blood, given in exchange for a life, that makes purification possible. (Leviticus 17:11 NLT)
>
> In fact, according to the law of Moses, nearly everything was purified with blood. For without the shedding of blood, there is no forgiveness. (Hebrews 9:22 NLT)

From Genesis throughout the Old Testament, we see the offering of animal sacrifices as a central part of God's relationship with His people. The blood from these sacrifices provided a temporary covering but didn't remove sin or its consequences. In the Exodus from Egypt, the blood of a lamb also protected the households of the Israelites when the death angel struck down all firstborns throughout the land.[38] All these were types and shadows of Jesus, the True Passover Lamb of God, whose blood was shed once and for all to take away humanity's sins and reconcile us to God.[39]

We must deeply appreciate the power of the blood of the cross of Jesus and exercise faith in what it has accomplished on our behalf. As you'll see later, part of the blueprint for becoming who you already are in Christ involves increasing your fellowship with the blood of Jesus through the Holy Communion.

Seven Places Jesus Shed His Blood

To increase our appreciation and faith, I'll share a snapshot of the seven places where Jesus shed His blood and what the blood from each place represented.[40]

1. *From the sweat of His forehead (Luke 22:44).* When Jesus prayed in the Garden of Gethsemane, His sweat fell to the ground like drops of blood. In that struggle, He surrendered His will to His heavenly Father. The first Adam exalted his will over God's in a Garden, and here, in another Garden, the Last Adam, Jesus, surrendered His will to God. In the droplets of this blood, there's victory over pain, suffering, and self-will. Jesus' blood falling to the ground broke the curse of toil and sweating imposed in Genesis 3:17-18.

2. *From the slaps and blows that disfigured His face (Matthew 26:67, Isaiah 52:14).* The face represents one's glory and self-image. Jesus allowed His physical identity to be beaten beyond recognition so our royal identity could be restored. In the droplets of this blood, there is victory over pride, rejection, humiliation, slander, and shame.

3. *From the pulling out of His beard (Isaiah 50:6).* The beard represents priesthood and honor. In the functional dimension of our royal identity, God created us to be a kingdom of priests.[41] In the droplets of this blood, there is redemption of the believer's priesthood. In this blood is the blessing of unity as described in Psalm 133:3, the restoration of honor, respect, and dignity to all, especially the male identity and biblical manhood.

4. *From the scourging of His back (Isaiah 53:4-5, Matthew 27:26).* The thirty-nine lashes that ripped through the flesh of Jesus' back represent the root of all diseases, sickness, and pain. In the droplets of this blood, we have victory over the spirit of infirmity, which is appropriated through the Holy Communion.[42]

5. *From the crown of thorns and beating in His head (Matthew 27:29-30).* Jesus endured the mockery of His kingship that ours might be restored. In the droplets of the blood that poured out from the pressing of the crown of thorns on His head, He gained victory over the devil's empire, and so did we. The foundation for the increase of His heavenly government on Earth was laid. In this blood, we also gain victory over strongholds of the mind and our thought life to secure sound mental and brain health. By wearing a crown of thorns, Jesus broke the spirit of poverty, toil, and sweating depicted by the thorns and thistles of Genesis 3:17-18.

6. *From the nails that pierced His hands and feet (Matthew 27:35, Isaiah 59:3, 6-7, 53:11).* Hands and feet represent one's work and destiny. In the droplets of this blood, Jesus gained victory for us over our sinful works and the crooked, twisted ways of generational iniquity. Jesus opened the way for us to again walk in paths of righteousness and be restored to proper spiritual order.

7. *From the spear that pierced His side (John 19:34).* The blood and water that gushed out when they pierced Jesus' side is said to be a sign that His heart was also pierced. In the droplets of this blood, a heart-to-heart relationship with God is restored. As Eve was taken from the side of Adam, the Bride of Christ (the Church) was birthed from His side. We also have victory and healing for broken hearts in this blood.

Jesus has restored our connection to God and His will through all this. He removed all barriers so our hearts could be knit together again in perfect union. Doesn't this detail put Jesus' shedding of His blood in a new light?

For me, it enlarged my faith and application of the blood of Jesus beyond an Easter-time focus. Releasing the power of the blood has become part of my day-to-day reality. The revelation of how God has united the Spirit and the blood to make it ceaselessly effective has made this reality even more personal. In his book, *The Blood of the Cross*, Andrew Murray reveals: "He [God] has so inseparably bound together the Holy Spirit and the blood that we may rely on Him to make the power of the blood ceaselessly effective in us by the power of the Spirit."[43]

Speaking about the Holy Spirit, Jesus said in John 16:14 AMPC, "He will honor and glorify Me, because He will take of (receive, draw upon) what is Mine and will reveal (declare, disclose, transmit) it to you." The Holy Spirit is ready and waiting to transmit all the power of the blood of Jesus to bring us forth in our royal identity.

The Great Exchange

Isaiah 61:1-3 is the prophetic announcement of the great exchange that Jesus was anointed to accomplish in resetting humanity's destiny back to God's original intent.

> The Spirit of the Sovereign Lord is on me, because the Lord has anointed me to proclaim good news to the poor. He has sent me to bind up the brokenhearted, to proclaim

freedom for the captives and release from darkness for the prisoners, to proclaim the year of the Lord's favor and the day of vengeance of our God, to comfort all who mourn, and provide for those who grieve in Zion—to bestow on them a crown of beauty instead of ashes, the oil of joy instead of mourning, and a garment of praise instead of a spirit of despair. They will be called oaks of righteousness, a planting of the Lord for the display of his splendor.

Isaiah 61:7 makes yet another announcement—a double portion exchange and everlasting joy: "Instead of your shame you will receive a double portion, and instead of disgrace you will rejoice in your inheritance. And so you will inherit a double portion in your land, and everlasting joy will be yours."

This great exchange is so powerful I need to itemize the points before moving on.

- Instead of ashes, a crown of beauty.
- Instead of mourning, the oil of joy.
- Instead of a spirit of despair, a garment of praise.
- Instead of ungodliness, we become oaks of righteousness to display God's glory.
- Instead of shame, a double portion.
- Instead of disgrace, rejoicing.
- Instead of loss, a double portion inheritance and everlasting joy.

All of this is ours by grace—undeserved, unmerited, and by the power of God working in us to do what we cannot do for ourselves. Let's now get to this place I call the Grace Exchange.

The Grace Exchange

My last book, *Ready. Set. Not Yet! Secrets for Teens about Sex* included a section about the Grace Exchange. The context was helping teenagers to see that the restoration of sexual wholeness is possible, regardless of past experiences. I'll share an excerpt here because we too, must access the Grace Exchange to reset our royal identity.

The trading floors of the stock exchanges around the world buzz with action when they're open for business. Well, God also has a trading floor that I call the Grace Exchange. It's open 24/7! You and I have the privilege of stepping onto God's trading floor at any time to "trade" with the blood of Jesus. It's not complicated at all. We go there with complete assurance that Jesus paid in full for all our sins. We can, therefore, be confident that God will not remember our past once we sincerely acknowledge what we've done, have a change of heart (that's what repentance is), and receive His forgiveness through the blood of Jesus.

God has a special place in this heavenly trading floor called the Throne of Grace (Hebrews 4:16). I often think of Him sitting there graciously waiting with His hand poised over the reset button. He gives an open invitation for you to come and trade in your past for the new beginning that Jesus purchased for you on the cross with His precious blood.

If you know about the factory reset of a Nintendo system or iPhone, then you understand what I mean. The old data is permanently deleted, the system is restored to original factory settings, and it starts to run like new.

If you haven't yet personally put your faith in what Jesus did at the cross for you, this is your opportunity. As you would have read earlier, we all shared Adam and Eve's experience and became like Humpty Dumpty. In addition to the legacy of sin inherited from Adam and Eve, we've also made our own choices that placed us at odds with God and left us desperately in need of a personal reset. Jesus poured out His lifeblood on the cross and paid in full for us to be put back together again. The Father raised Jesus from the dead so you can have a new spiritual life by faith in Him.

Jesus is the only One who makes a complete reset possible. There are two simple steps to a complete personal reset. First, believe in your heart that Jesus died for you. Second, confirm your faith with your words. This simple prayer will help you to do that: "Dear Jesus, I ask you to reset my life [and royal identity]. I'm sorry for going against God's way. Thank you for dying on the cross for me. I now choose to follow you as my Saviour and Lord. I open the door of my heart and receive you now. Thank you for the gift of forgiveness, my new life, and the relationship I now share with you, the Father and the Holy Spirit. Amen."

It's done! You said that prayer in faith and an instant spiritual transaction occurred. You have a new beginning, even if you don't feel any different. The Father wiped your slate completely clean with the blood of Jesus. Every violation against God has been removed, and you are free from them. Welcome to your clean, new slate!

You have just experienced a new spiritual birth and are now a new creation in Christ. The Spirit of God has given you new spiritual life. The totality of who you are as a royal offspring of God has been restored to you. Something powerful to know is that the blood of Jesus speaks continually on your behalf in the Grace Exchange. Hebrews 11:24 says the blood of Jesus speaks a better word concerning you. It speaks of reconciliation, redemption, grace, mercy, love, peace, joy, and more.

Interrupting the Interruption

Since this chapter is the flipside of Chapter 4, where we discussed five areas of interruption of our royal identity blueprint, it's important to see how the reset and exchange accomplished by the blood of the cross of Jesus affected these areas.

Relational Reconciliation

Reconciled is such a heartwarming word in the context of relationships. Colossians 1:20 says God reconciled everything to Himself, including our relationship bonds. Our broken relational capacity was exchanged for the divine nature of peace, which is more than the absence of strife. It is wholeness and completion within ourselves and with others. Ephesians 2:13-14 affirms, "But now in Christ Jesus you who once were far away have been brought near by the blood of Christ. For he himself is our peace, who has made the two groups one and has destroyed the barrier, the dividing wall of hostility."

Think outside the box momentarily and imagine the impact of God reconciling all things unto himself. Enmity is broken and replaced by divine harmony—restored to innocence again, original intent as if the interruption of God's creation design had never happened. This relationship reconciliation has reconnected us to God as our Source and makes wholesome relationships with each other possible.

Fatherhood of God Restored

In John 20:17, Jesus announced to Mary at His resurrection: "Do not hold on to me, for I have not yet ascended to the Father. Go instead to my brothers and tell them, 'I am ascending to my Father and your Father, to my God and your God.'" Those words, "to my Father and your Father," are like a breath of fresh air. Go ahead and take it in!

Through the blood of Jesus, we experience new spiritual birth, whereby alienation and estrangement from God as our Source and heavenly Father are exchanged for the restoration of our divine lineage. John 1:12-13 affirms, "Yet to all who did receive him, to those who believed in his name, he gave the right to become children of God—children born not of natural descent, nor of human decision or a husband's will, but born of God."

The blood of the cross of Jesus removed all barriers to our sense of belonging and acceptance. Moreover, the Spirit of the Firstborn Royal Son comes to indwell us to bring us into a fuller relationship with the Father. "Because you are his sons, God sent the Spirit of his Son into our hearts, the Spirit who calls out, "*Abba*, Father." So you are no longer a slave, but God's child; and since you are his child, God has made you also an heir." (Galatians 4:6-7)

Righteousness and Glory Restored

Jesus exchanged our sin (the totality of the nature of sin) for His righteousness and our nakedness and shame for His glory. These verses sum up the exchange.

> God made him who had no sin to be sin for us, so that in him we might become the righteousness of God. (2 Corinthians 5:21)
>
> In bringing many sons and daughters to glory, it was fitting that God, for whom and through whom everything exists, should make the pioneer of their salvation perfect through what he suffered. (Hebrews 2:10)

Jesus' blood mediated a new covenant on our behalf, and He fulfilled all the requirements of the old covenant, which were based on works. Righteousness, attained by works under the old covenant, became a gift that couldn't be earned. Romans 5:17 beautifully explains the reset: "For if, by the trespass of the one man, death reigned through that one man, how much more will those who receive God's abundant provision of grace and of the gift of righteousness reign in life through the one man, Jesus Christ!"

The blood of Jesus provided complete cleansing. Jesus became our gift of righteousness to reign in life and the hope of glory alive in us.

Kingdom Migration

"Let them have dominion" is God's overarching vocational purpose for humanity's existence. In the Kingdom mutiny that Satan staged in the Garden of Eden, he usurped our dominion authority, became the god or ruler of this world, and brought us under his dominion of darkness.

Colossians 1:13-14 NLT describes the great Kingdom migration or transfer that Jesus accomplished by the blood of His cross: "For he has rescued us from the kingdom of darkness and transferred us into the Kingdom of his dear Son, who purchased our freedom and forgave our sins." This rescue and transfer put us back where we belong and restored the Kingdom authority that Satan had usurped.

Keys represent authority and, as Jesus said in Matthew 16:19, He has given us the keys of His Kingdom: "I will give you the keys of the kingdom of heaven; whatever you bind on earth will be bound in heaven, and whatever you loose on earth will be loosed in heaven." Luke 10:19 TPT describes Jesus' delegation of authority in beautiful, faith-inspiring language: "Now you understand that I have imparted to you my authority to trample over his kingdom. You will trample upon every demon before you and overcome every power Satan possesses. Absolutely nothing will harm you as you walk in this authority."

By resetting God's original commission to humanity and reinstating our authority, Jesus made the way for the Great Commission recorded in Mark 16:16-18 and Matthew 28:19-20. The original Genesis commission was a seedbed, and its reinstatement made the Great Commission of the New Testament possible.

The Exodus of the Children of Israel out of Egypt foreshadowed our migration out of Satan's dominion. Just as they couldn't take any baggage with them, neither can we. We are made new creations, and everything old (from being under Satan's dominion) has to be put off and left behind. King Saul's hiding in the baggage at his coronation reminds us to leave the baggage of our old creation self and its accumulations behind.

Soul Power Reset

We were never made to be ruled by the realm of the soul. However, the spiritual death Adam and Eve experienced when they ate from the Tree of Knowledge caused the exaltation of the soul (mind, emotions, and will).

Instead of the spirit-led beings God created us to be, we became soul-dominated. In bringing everything back to its original intent by the blood of His cross, Jesus made provision for the soul to be reset under the spirit's control. However, it is important to note that while the spirit experiences instant rebirth, reset, and elevation when we become born again, the soul does not. Resetting the soul under the spirit's control requires an ongoing transformation process.

Second Corinthians 5:17 says, "Therefore, if anyone is in Christ, the new creation has come: The old has gone, the new is here!" Translations of this verse that use the expression "all things becoming new" have led to some misunderstanding. Many believers fail to recognize that while their spirit has already been made brand new, their soul is becoming new only to the extent that it relinquishes its control and receives the life of the spirit. In other words, our soul has to go through the process of unbecoming what it became in the Fall to become new like our spirit. You may have heard it said this way: our spirit has been saved, but our soul is being saved. That's why James 1:21 NLT gives this instruction: "So get rid of all the filth and evil in your lives, and humbly accept the word God has planted in your hearts, for it has the power to save your souls."

God gave humanity the gift of free will at creation. Therefore, it means an element of choice is involved in resetting soul power. If God had automatically reset the soul as He did the spirit, it would have violated our free will. We have a significant role in getting back to royalty.

The blood of the cross of Jesus has reversed every interruption to God's original creation design. Coming forth in our royal identity hinges on our choices to apprehend all that Jesus has accomplished to bring us back to where we belong. The question is, will the royal you come forth?

Reflection and Action

What insights did you gain from this chapter?

_____

_____

_____

_____

Specify at least two actions you'll take based on the insights gained.

1. _____

   _____

2. _____

   _____

CHAPTER 13

WILL THE ROYAL YOU PLEASE COME FORTH!

*Authenticity is the daily practice of letting go of who
we think we're supposed to be and embracing who we are.*

– Brené Brown

In the 1970s and 1980s, there was a popular Television Game Show called To Tell the Truth. It may have been before your time, so let me tell you how it worked. Each episode featured three participants and a group of celebrity panelists. The participants included a central character and two challengers or imposters. All three participants identified themselves by the same name (for example, Michael Smith). However, only the central character was the real Michael Smith. The show host would read the central character's biography, after which the panelists took turns questioning all three participants.

In answering the questions, the two imposters were allowed to lie, but the central character always had to answer truthfully. At the end of the questioning round, the panelists voted for who they thought was the real Michael Smith. Then came the moment of truth with a final question from the host: "Will the real Michael Smith please stand up?" After a few faking gestures from the participants, the real Michael Smith stood up. The show ended with the imposters revealing their names and occupations and receiving monetary awards based on how many panelists had voted for them.

These shows were quite entertaining when I watched them years ago. However, after being commissioned on my identity assignment by the Lord, I realized that consciously or subconsciously, Hollywood was using satire to reflect humanity's identity crisis. The show provided entertainment but no solutions. Laughter is good medicine, but we don't want it to be at the expense of humanity's brokenness.

Come Forth in Your Royal Identity is designed to accomplish what the game show couldn't do: to reveal the royal you that God created and empower you to come forth. Here is a good place for a pause. Grab a mirror or stand in front of one. Look at yourself in the mirror, and invite the real you to come forth (insert your name in the blank). Unlike the game show, you're not framing your invitation as a question. You're speaking a gentle command: "Will the royal _____ please come forth!

That's a defining moment right there. Your journey into royalty is about to accelerate, and I join my faith with yours, cheering you along.

I'll use the rest of the chapter to reframe four of Jesus' miracle encounters from an identity perspective. The first is Lazarus' resurrection. Second, the healing of the lame man at the pool of Bethesda. Third, the recovery of blind Bartimaeus' sight. Fourth, the healing of the woman in the synagogue. These miracles required faith action: direct human participation, intense desire, or cooperation with Jesus.

Loose Him, and Let Him Go!

As you're aware, Jesus' command in raising Lazarus from the dead (Lazarus come forth!) inspired the title of the book. The account of John 11 tells us that the participation of others before and after the command was like two bookends in this miracle. Lazarus' tomb was a cave with a stone rolled across its entrance. Jesus didn't immediately command Lazarus to come forth when he arrived at the tomb. First, He instructed the people to roll away the stone then He prayed. His instruction was intentional. Lazarus' sisters and the mourners had to break their mental agreement with the belief that it was too late for Lazarus to be raised from the dead. He activated their faith for the miracle by having them remove the stone.

Lazarus responded to Jesus' command. He came forth bound in grave clothes. The language of John 11:44 NKJV is precise—"And he who had died came out bound hand and foot with graveclothes, and his face was wrapped with a cloth. Jesus said to them, "Loose him, and let him go."

Take note. Lazarus came out of the grave, but his resurrection back to life was incomplete until the grave clothes were removed. Again, for this phase of the miracle, Jesus needed the participation of the family and mourners. Lazarus' spirit had responded, but he needed to be physically loosed. I am aware that it was the custom of the culture to wrap the face of the dead with cloth. However, I find it significant from an identity perspective because the face represents one's glory and self-image. It is possible that even as born-again believers (resurrected), our glory is veiled, and the veil has to be removed. We need unveiled faces to behold the glory of God and be transformed into His likeness.

> And we all, who with **unveiled faces** contemplate the Lord's glory, are being transformed into his image with ever-increasing glory, which comes from the Lord, who is the Spirit. (2 Corinthians 3:18, emphasis added)

Coming forth in our royal identity will likely need the support of others to remove our grave clothes (fig leaves). The help needed will look different for different people. As I said before, based on personal experience and the experience of others, the help may include professional counseling. You have permission to get the help you need. Many individuals are being set free by realizing there's no competition or conflict between faith in Jesus, counseling, or even medication to help stabilize their mental health.

Do You Want to Be Made Well?

In John 5:1-15, we meet a man at the pool of Bethesda who had been lame for 38 years. He is among many sick people waiting for the water to be supernaturally stirred so they can go into the pool and be healed. When Jesus saw the man and realized he had been lame for a long time, he asked him a question—"Do you want to be made well?" (John 5:6 NKJV)

As you can imagine, after being paralyzed for 38 years, this man's condition had become his way of life, his identity. You'll recall from Chapter 3 that questions are God's GPS that He uses to help us locate ourselves. He uses them for self-awareness. They help us become aware of our desires and the true condition of our hearts. As it was for Adam, who was hiding, the purpose of Jesus' question was to bring the lame man to a place of honesty with himself. Had he settled for living in the paralyzed state, or did He really want to be well? On the surface, it seemed like a rhetorical question because the whole point of being at the pool was for an opportunity to be healed. Jesus looked beyond what was apparent and spoke to the man's heart.

The man replied that he had no one to help him into the water. Someone would always get ahead of him while he tried to get in. Jesus followed up the man's response with a command: Get up! Pick up your mat and walk!" The result was instant. John 5:8-9 reads, "Jesus said to him, "Rise, take up your bed and walk." And immediately the man was made well, took up his bed, and walked."

What happened? Jesus wouldn't have imposed something on the man he wasn't ready for. His strategy was to first heal the man's belief by breaking his mental agreement with the adopted identity that he'd always be lame. Jesus' command called forth a visible faith action as evidence that the man would no longer settle for living in this condition.

As you read through this book, I pray that if you have settled for a fig leaf identity because of negative circumstances that seem impossible to change, you will break that mental agreement. May Jesus' question and command be catalysts to activate the faith action you need to come forth in your royal identity: Do you want to be made well? Rise! Take authority over that condition or circumstance and walk out of it. It does not define who you are.

Lord, I Want to See

The Gospels of Matthew, Mark, and Luke include accounts of Jesus restoring sight to blind men. Mark is unique in naming the blind beggar Bartimaeus. When Bartimaeus heard that Jesus was approaching, he started shouting. In addressing Jesus, he revealed the depth of his hope and faith: "Jesus, Son of David, have mercy on me." Those around tried to quiet him, but he shouted even more. Bartimaeus wasn't just a desperate man. He was tired of his condition and circumstances.

You read earlier that our circumstances and needs are factors that help to shape distorted identities. Gideon, for example, had an adopted identity based on the tribe he was from and the victimization of the raiding Midianites. Illnesses, trauma, and shame can also form invisible mantles and be worn as an identity. Blind Bartimaeus had a physical cloak that identified him as a beggar. However, something within him knew that wasn't his real identity. Why do I say that? When he heard that Jesus had called him, Mark 10:50 reports, "Throwing his cloak aside, he jumped to his feet and came to Jesus."

That's what you call actioning your faith! His physical sight hadn't yet been restored, but he determined he would no longer need a beggar's cloak. His eyes of faith had seen the real Bartimaeus, and he wasn't a blind beggar. "I want to see" wasn't just the expected response from a blind person who was asked what he wanted. He was a beggar and could have asked for money or food to sustain His condition. Bartimaeus' words were loaded with the boldness and confidence of someone who knew it was their time to come forth and leave their limitations behind. Jesus commended his faith as the catalyst for his healing. The first word of Jesus' response, "Go," was a command with force equivalent to the command that called Lazarus to come forth.

Malachi 4:2-3 NLT is rising in my spirit as a prophetic announcement from the Lord to you: "But for you who fear my name, the Sun of Righteousness will rise with healing in his wings. And you will go free, leaping with joy like calves let out to pasture. On the day when I act, you will tread upon the wicked as if they were dust under your feet, says the LORD of Heaven's Armies."

Come forth! Go free! Leap with joy! Tread upon every distorted identity; they're dust under your feet!

Woman, Thou Art Loosed

From this woman's story in Luke 13, Bishop T. D. Jakes began an international movement that has helped thousands of women transcend their painful past. If you've read his best-selling book or attended a Woman Thou Art Loosed conference, you're all too familiar with this powerful, miraculous encounter. For those who may not be, let me share a few highlights.

Unlike the previous three encounters, Jesus met this woman in a religious setting—the synagogue on a Sabbath day. (That's the equivalent of the Church on a Sunday). A spirit of infirmity had crippled her, and for eighteen years, she was bent over, unable to straighten herself. Can you imagine being in a condition where dirt is all you see day in and day out? Like the lame man at the pool and blind Bartimaeus, her condition was ideal for distorting her beliefs about herself.

This woman may have settled for the way things were. I have often wondered whether everyone else had also resolved that her condition would never change because it was too late and too far gone. Luke 13:12-13 placed Jesus on the scene, and everything changed. "But when Jesus saw her, He called her to Him and said to her, "Woman, you are loosed from your infirmity." And He laid His hands on her, and immediately she was made straight, and glorified God." (NKJV)

Imagine the joy! Seeing the face of Jesus and everything else she hadn't seen for eighteen years. While the angry response of the synagogue leader is surprising, in some respects, it's not. His loyalty to the law exceeded his compassion. (We'll touch on that in a moment). There's something Jesus said in verse sixteen that's very relevant for you and me as believers in Christ. "Then should not this woman, a daughter of Abraham whom Satan has kept bound for eighteen long years, be set free on the Sabbath day from what bound her?"

In referring to the woman as a daughter of Abraham, Jesus established that she had a right to be free from what bound her because of her covenant relationship with God through Abraham. Whether male or female, we can appeal to the same covenantal right because of what Galatians 3:29 says: "If you belong to Christ, then you are Abraham's seed, and heirs according to the promise." Moreover, the promises of our new covenant with God through Jesus are superior, as Hebrews 8:6 tells us, "But in fact the ministry Jesus has received is as superior to theirs as the covenant of which he is mediator is superior to the old one, since the new covenant is established on better promises."

The ultimate reset and exchange that Jesus accomplished on our behalf obtained our freedom from everything that would limit us from coming forth in our royal identity. The freedom is now ours to apprehend!

Common Denominators

Some similarities emerge from these encounters. They are noteworthy for coming forth in your royal identity. First, faith is a prerequisite. You can be sure that God loves you too much to leave you as you are. He will come alongside and empower you for faith action as He did for the lame man at the pool. Second, you will need to break mental agreement with any condition, circumstance, need, or belief that's an obstacle to you coming forth. Third, your coming forth will cause you and others to experience unprecedented dimensions of glorifying and praising God. That's a motivating force right there! Finally, in all four encounters,

Jesus experienced fierce retaliation from the religious order for the healing and freedom He brought to people. Religion will not help you to come forth in your royal identity. You need an encounter with Jesus that will transform you. The Christian faith is based on a relationship with Jesus Christ, not loyalty to religious laws and customs. Be mindful that outward conformity to standards without inner transformation is a setup for distorted identities.

Rest assured that Jesus has seen you, and as He called Lazarus, Bartimaeus, and the woman in the synagogue, He is calling you forth into royalty. May you have the faith, courage, boldness, and persistence of Bartimaeus to defy all the odds. Give yourself permission to get the help you need to remove anything from your life that's symbolized by Lazarus' grave clothes.

In the next chapter, we will go a little deeper for more insight into obstacles that could hinder the royal you from coming forth.

Reflection and Action

What insights did you gain from this chapter?

_____
_____
_____
_____

Specify at least two actions you'll take based on the insights gained.

1. _____
_____

2. _____
_____

CHAPTER 14

WHAT'S HOLDING YOU BACK?

*Not by might nor by power, but by my Spirit,
says the Lord Almighty.*

— Zechariah 4:6

Typically, in seeking solutions to a problem, we tend to focus on whatever is most obvious. That's fine, provided we recognize that the obvious may be symptoms of a bigger issue. We may just be seeing the tip of an iceberg. Getting to what's beneath the surface is necessary for long-lasting solutions. When I first wrote this chapter, I had a list of the obstacles that could hinder us from coming forth in our royal identity. The list included denial, fear, a stronghold of lies, negative experiences and thoughts, shame, unresolved issues, guilt, self-condemnation, and blaming others. I found plenty of relevant information in my unpublished manuscript that I could copy. But the Holy Spirit (my Writing Coach) wouldn't release me to do that. His instruction was simple: "Get to the root!"

It's not that these factors aren't legitimate. They are. We all need to be aware of them and how they manifest in our lives. I realized, however, that many of them are symptoms. That means they'll linger or return if we only deal with the presented needs or crises. But their power would be dismantled if we resolved the root cause. I waited for more insight. The Holy Spirit revealed what was already right before my eyes. This root cause is what interrupted God's original creation design and intent. I had identified it in laying the foundation for the book in the early chapters. Threads of its expression have been running through every chapter. Are you figuring out what it is? The Tree of Knowledge of Good and Evil. More precisely, the effects that eating from the Tree of Knowledge had on our soul is the root cause of what's holding us back from coming forth in our royal identity.

In His ultimate reset and exchange through the blood of His cross, Jesus interrupted Satan's interruptions and put us back where we belonged. However, you'll recall that we ended Chapter 12 by saying that coming forth in our royal identity hinges on our choices to apprehend all that Jesus has accomplished. This chapter is dedicated to the most critical choice we must make concerning the Tree of Knowledge of Good and Evil and the realm from which it operates, our soul.

The Holy Spirit's Ministry is Essential

Our key verse of Zechariah 4:6 alerts us to how vital it is to rely on the Holy Spirit's power in overcoming barriers to coming forth in our royal identity. Our coming forth will require faith action, as you saw in the encounters from the last chapter. For these faith actions, we'll need the empowerment of the Holy Spirit. We also need Him to guide us into truth and bring the manifestation of what Jesus has accomplished for us.

From the perspective of coming forth in our royal identity, let's look at what Jesus revealed to His disciples in John 16 about the essential work of the Holy Spirit.

> But when the truth-giving Spirit comes, **he will unveil the reality of every truth within you**. He won't speak on his own, but only what he hears from the Father, and he will reveal prophetically to you what is to come. He will glorify me on the earth, for **he will receive from me what is mine and reveal it to you**. Everything that belongs to the Father belongs to me—that's why I say that the Divine Encourager will receive what is mine and reveal it to you. (John 16:13-15 TPT, emphasis added)

I hold these verses very close to my heart as a reminder that without the Holy Spirit, I'm settling for self-reliance (a fruit of the Tree of Knowledge) and shortchanging myself. So my prayer is: Come, Holy Spirit. Move upon me, in me, and through me. By your power, reveal truth, disclose and manifest the royal image of Christ into my whole spirit, soul, and body.

There are Still Two Trees

As we focus on the Tree of Knowledge, let's also recap a few important truths to get to the heart of what's holding back the royal you from coming forth.

When Adam and Eve ate from the Tree of Knowledge of Good and Evil, they ingested its root system (DNA) into their being. Specifically, the Tree of Knowledge became the source that fueled the soul's new posture of autonomy. The spirit had been separated from God as its Source, and the soul (with its faculties of mind, emotions, and will) became dominant. Although God had covered Adam and Eve with the bloody skin of an animal, the consequences of their violation remained intact. By shedding His blood and offering Himself on the cross, Jesus became the perfect sacrifice that removed humanity's sins, transgressions, and iniquity.

Just as an element of choice (free will) was instrumental in Adam and Eve's violation, it's also required in the remedy. So, Jesus chose to offer Himself as the perfect sacrifice, and we also have a choice in accepting His sacrifice. Our spirit receives new life when we accept Jesus as our sacrificial offering to God. When we make this choice, Jesus as the Life-Giving Spirit and the True Vine (Tree of Life) indwells our spirit as its Source.[44] In other words, Jesus becomes installed within our spirit as the spiritual power to dislodge and supersede the DNA of the Tree of Knowledge in the soul. This life in our reborn spirit includes the reality of our royal identity. Colossians 1:27 describes this reality as Christ in you, the hope of glory.

Here are two keys we don't want to miss.

First, at our initial salvation experience, each believer again becomes a Garden of Eden with two trees at the center. We find ourselves at Genesis 2:9b all over again: "In the middle of the garden were the tree of life and the tree of the knowledge of good and evil."

Second, God's command of Genesis 2:17 applies as much to us as it did to Adam: "But you must not eat from the tree of the knowledge of good and evil, for when you eat from it, you will certainly die." The dimension of spiritual "death" we experience when we eat from the Tree of Knowledge as believers prevents the life of God in our spirit from flowing into the rest of our being.

So there are still two trees in the garden. Which tree are you eating from? Until the power source of the Tree of Knowledge is dismantled and our soul is surrendered to the spirit, we're set on automatic pilot. By default, we eat from the Tree of Knowledge. On the other hand, eating from the Tree of Life requires deliberate, intentional action. As the Scripture tells us, however, the soul (flesh) wars against the spirit, sabotaging our choices.

> I do not understand what I do. For what I want to do I do not do, but what I hate I do. For I do not do the good I want to do, but the evil I do not want to do—this I keep on doing. (Romans 7:15,19)

The Apostle Paul wrote these words as a born-again believer. He alerted us to the battle between the soul (flesh) and spirit—the battle between the two trees every believer faces. At the end of the chapter, he describes these two forces as opposing laws but ends on the hopeful note of victory in Christ. Let's read these verses.

> So I find this law at work: Although I want to do good, evil is right there with me. For in my inner being I delight in God's law; but I see another law at work in me, waging war against the law of my mind and making me a prisoner of the law of sin at work within me. What a wretched man I am! Who will rescue me from this body that is subject to death? Thanks be to God, who delivers me through Jesus Christ our Lord! (Romans 7:21-25)

I'm sure you got the point. The Tree of Knowledge will sabotage our desires and efforts to come forth in our royal identity. Its resistance is formidable and has to be overcome. The question is how? We chose to give the Tree of Knowledge its power of autonomy through Adam and Eve, so it also requires our intentional, ongoing choice to break its root system and dominance in our soul.

What does that look like? We must release ourselves from the Tree of Knowledge of Good and Evil. Denounce any attachment to it, and declare as Jesus did to the fig tree that we will not eat fruit from it again. Have you ever prayed that kind of prayer? (Ephesians 6:18 says we're to pray with all kinds of prayer). The Holy Spirit showed me the need for this detachment prayer only a few years ago. This kind of prayer has since become an integral part of my preparation each time I partake of the Holy Communion. We'll pray this prayer together at the end of the chapter.

There's an offshoot or outgrowth of the Tree of Knowledge we must safeguard against. It's the Spirit of Religion. As you saw in the last chapter, the Pharisees and other religious leaders couldn't share Heaven's joy with those who had broken free from their limitations. But you were not made for religion. You were made for a life-giving relationship with Father God through Jesus Christ. Religion tries to perform (work) its way into acceptance by God. That's not for you! As Colossians 1:6 KJV says, you're already accepted in the Beloved, Jesus Christ.

Psuche Won't Let You Go

When I heard this expression many years ago, I instantly responded, "Who on earth is Psuche?" Contrary to my initial thoughts, I eventually realized Psuche isn't another name for Satan or for the Pharaoh of Egypt, who had refused to let God's people go. My knowledge of Greek was non-existent then, so I had no idea that *psuche* is the word for soul.

We have established that in the Fall of humanity the soul exalted its will over God's and became the dominant power in place of our spirit. This condition of an exalted soul is reproduced in everyone. We're all born with a soul that eventually exalts itself above God. Only when we come to faith in Christ and our spirit is regenerated with the life of God is the capacity of our spirit to lead restored. However, the problem is that the soul refuses to concede. You've heard of dictatorial political leaders who refuse to relinquish power after losing an election. The soul behaves like that after our spirit is regenerated as a new creation in Christ.

Although Jesus was the Son of God, living as a spirit-led man on Earth, He had to overcome the soul's attempts at exalting itself over God's will. He experienced it at the start of His ministry when Satan tempted Him in the wilderness to operate outside of God's authority.[45] Another occasion was when Peter reprimanded Him for saying He would die and be raised again. Jesus recognized that the source from which Peter was speaking was his soul. This was the same voice that had said to Eve, "You shall not surely die." Satan had inspired Peter to sidetrack Jesus from His mission. Jesus' rebuke of Peter and what He said to the disciples let us know that His mission was to gain victory over the soul by taking it to the cross.

> But He turned and said to Peter, "Get behind Me, Satan! You are an offense to Me, for you are not mindful of the things of God, but the things of men." Then Jesus said to His disciples, "If anyone desires to come after Me, let him deny himself, and take up his cross, and follow Me. For

whoever desires to save his **life** will lose it, but whoever loses his **life** for My sake will find it. For what profit is it to a man if he gains the whole world, and loses his own **soul**? Or what will a man give in exchange for his **soul**? (Matthew 16:23-26 NKJV, emphasis added)

The meaning of these verses is veiled unless we understand that each reference to life and soul is the same Greek word, *psuche*. In other instances, when Jesus spoke of finding life eternal, He used a different word for life, *zoe*. For example, in John 12:25: "Anyone who loves their life [*psuche*] will lose it, while anyone who hates their life [*psuche*] in this world will keep it for eternal life [*zoe*]." Although Jesus' soul was not defiled, His mission was to accomplish a soul exchange at the cross—His undefiled soul for our defiled soul. By gaining victory over the soul through the cross, we could follow Jesus and experience the same victory.

In the Garden of Gethsemane, just before His crucifixion, Jesus had His final battle with the soul. His soul wrestled to find another way to save humanity. The intensity of the battle was so great that Luke 22:44 says, "And being in anguish, he prayed more earnestly, and his sweat was like drops of blood falling to the ground." By the grace of God, Jesus' spirit triumphed over the will of His soul, and He surrendered to the Father's authority: "My Father, if it is possible, may this cup be taken from me. Yet not as I will, but as you will." (Matthew 26:39b)

Earlier in Chapter 12, you read that this was the first of seven places where Jesus shed His blood. Here's what Ana Mendez-Ferrell reveals about the blood from Jesus' sweat. "Victory over all pain and suffering of the soul is found in those drops in the sweat of His forehead. The power that submits our will to God is found there. We can drink those same drops, and make any desire that opposes God to submit to Him... They attract angels to help us die to ourselves."[46] With this revelation, we can appropriate this specific dimension of the blood of Jesus when we partake of the Holy Communion.

If Jesus' undefiled soul put up such a fight before His crucifixion, can you imagine what our fallen soul will do? It will fight every effort of ours to take it to the cross. That's why we noted upfront that only the Spirit of God can accomplish this in us.

Matthew 16:24 NKJV, which we read earlier, records these words from Jesus: "If anyone desires to come after Me . . ." Let's unpack those words in the context of coming forth in our royal identity. Jesus is the Firstborn

Royal Son in whose image we are made and are being conformed. Our conformity to His image also amounts to "coming after him" (not just following Him as a disciple). Experiencing this reality requires bringing our soul to the cross so our spirit life can come forth. Our royal identity is spirit-derived, so coming forth in our royal identity is through our regenerated spirit and surrendered soul.

Like Pharaoh in Egypt, who said he'd let God's people go, then reversed his decision ten times, Psuche will cause us to think that we're breaking free from distorted identities but end up holding us back. Pharaoh finally conceded with the tenth plague God sent, the death of Egypt's firstborns. Even so, he and his troops relentlessly pursued the Children of Israel up to the Red Sea crossing. That's a picture of Psuche in operation. As the Red Sea brought death to Pharaoh and his troops, the cross was also designed to bring death to Psuche.

It's important to know that memories stored in our subconscious mind and brain are what Psuche uses to control us. That's where the root system of the Tree of Knowledge is established. By breaking our agreement with and our attachment to this source, we overcome the power of Psuche to hold us back. We're going to pray into that right now.

Prayer of Release from the Tree of Knowledge

Heavenly Father, thank you for the blood of Jesus that gives me access to your presence. I come boldly to your throne of grace, washed and cleansed by His precious blood. Father, I have come to trade my attachment and loyalty to the Tree of Knowledge of Good and Evil and activate a new and vital union with the Tree of Life in its place.

On behalf of myself and generations past, I repent all the way back to Adam for having chosen to eat from the Tree of Knowledge of Good and Evil. I confess that consciously and unconsciously, our unsurrendered soul has continued eating from this forbidden tree. Against you, Lord God Almighty, have we sinned and done this evil in your sight. Grant us forgiveness, we pray. And as you have promised, be merciful to our unrighteousness and remember our sins and lawless deeds no more.

Let the heavens and Earth bear record this day that, in the Name of Jesus, I permanently denounce all attachments to the Tree of Knowledge of Good and Evil as my source. Based on the ultimate reset of the blood of the cross of Jesus and by the power of the Holy Spirit working in me, I choose to release myself from the Tree of Knowledge completely. I denounce the spirit of independence and the right to determine for myself what's right or wrong, good or evil. Father, I surrender to your sovereign authority.

I ask for the power of your Word, your Blood, and your Spirit to dismantle the DNA of the Tree of Knowledge and its dominance over my soul. Let any associated altars that have knowingly or unknowingly been erected be demolished by the fire of God. Now, Lord, restore your holy altar for me to worship you only. I choose to take up the cross daily and surrender to its crucifying power in my soul. I embrace the victory of the cross as a permanent filter between me and the Tree of Knowledge. Let the blood of Jesus be applied to cleanse my mind, emotions, will, and heart of all impressions left by the Tree of Knowledge and other harmful experiences, and let them be remembered no more.

Now, Father, by the power of your Holy Spirit, I choose to reattach the totality of my being to the Tree of Life. As a branch living in vital union with the True Vine, let the life of your Spirit fill my spirit through and through, flood my soul, and saturate my body. Restore your perfect divine order in me as it was in the beginning. Thank you for bringing me back to yourself, back to your original intent, back to innocence again. In Heaven's authority, I echo the words that Jesus spoke to the fig tree: "Let no one eat fruit from you ever again." In the Name of Jesus, it is so.

I speak to my soul to receive the grace of God in every faculty — mind, emotions, and will. Soul, I bless you to function as the fully integrated, spirit-led, and divinely ordered entity that God created you to be. Receive now the engrafted Word of God, which is able to save you. Rest and trust in God, who works in you to accomplish His good purpose for you. My soul, your day of rejoicing has come! Magnify the Lord! Victory is yours in Jesus' Name. Hallelujah and Amen![47]

Selah.

Pause for a few moments in God's presence. Rest in Him and receive His life flow.

James 5:16b KJV says, "The effectual fervent prayer of a righteous man availeth much." So, for reinforcement, I encourage you to pray this prayer regularly with thanksgiving. It's foundational for the ongoing transformation of our souls.

The ultimate benefit of laying down our soul (*psuche*) life is that we experience living by the eternal quality of spirit life as God intended. It's in this spirit life that we discover and experience who we really are. The next chapter explores why the coming forth of the royal you is significant. You'll be motivated by what you discover.

Reflection and Action

What insights did you gain from this chapter?

_____

_____

_____

_____

Specify at least two actions you'll take based on the insights gained.

1. _____

_____

2. _____

_____

CHAPTER 15

THE SIGNIFICANCE OF THE ROYAL YOU

*Understanding your identity in Christ is absolutely
essential for living a victorious life.*

– Neil Anderson

A little motivation goes a long way. I remember many of the workshops and seminars I attended in the corporate world. One thing differentiated the facilitators that got and held my attention. They'd include the WIIFM (What's In It For Me) concept in their seminar overview. We're wired to perk up when we know the benefit we will receive from something.

Well, coming forth in your royal identity is a win-win-win. It's a win for you. It's a win for God. And it's a win for others. You need you. God needs you. And others need you. God created the royal you as an original masterpiece to fulfill a unique purpose. God does His best work in and through originals. He won't settle for anything less. Your glory is in the real you. Anything that's not authentic is a counterfeit, a fake, an imitation, or a knockoff, as they'd say in today's fashion lingo. That's what the distorted fig leaf identities are, so we're not settling for them. We refuse to be anything less than the original royal masterpiece that we are.

The significance of the royal you is that it comes with heavenly and earthly benefits. We'll be highlighting seven benefits to underscore the importance of coming forth in your royal identity:

1. You make God joyful.
2. You enjoy peace and reign in life.
3. You operate in spiritual authority.
4. You pray bold prayers.
5. You advance God's Kingdom purposes.
6. You display God's glory.
7. You become a generational legacy builder.

You Make God Joyful

Joyfulness may not be the first emotional attribute we ascribe to God. Yet, as the Source of our joy, He is full of joy. I'm not overreaching when I say that God's greatest joy and delight was the creation of His family of human offspring. In the record of creation, in five instances, Genesis gives us the same appraisal of the work that had been done: "And God saw that it was good."[48] However, after creating humankind to embody His image and likeness, Genesis 1:31 records a superior assessment: "God saw all that he had made, and it was very good." Very good, underscores the depth of joy God experienced in bringing us forth.

Imagine the joy of parents at the birth of their newborn. Imagine their hope and dreams of what that child will become. God experienced all that and more. As parents, we are hurt and sorrowful when our children lose their way in life. After seeing the depravity of humanity in Noah's time, Genesis 6:6 NLT says, "So the LORD was sorry he had ever made them and put them on the earth. It broke his heart." I used the NLT translation because the language is precise. God wasn't just deeply troubled or grieved that His prized creation had fallen to such decadence. It broke His heart!

We rejoice that God didn't abandon the work of His hands, although He had all reason to do so. Instead, He emptied Heaven and sent into the corrupt world the perfect image and mold from which we were originally made, Jesus Christ. In a sense, God went back to the drawing board. And through the redemptive work of the blood of the cross of Jesus, God brought forth a new creation. Get this! It's not a small thing when we affirm, according to Second Corinthians 5:17, that we are a new creation in Christ.

Now, here's the clincher. Coming forth in our royal identity will fill God's heart with even greater joy than at the original creation. Why? Creating us in His image and likeness was God's love gift to us. Our choice to accept His redemptive royal identity in Christ is our love gift to Him.

If you've been around me for any time, you may have heard me say, I live to see a smile on my Father's face. Coming forth in our royal identity will make Him joyful. Let's do it!

You Enjoy Peace and Reign in Life

You and I would like nothing more than a peaceful life. Often, we think of peace as the absence of strife, but biblical peace is a whole lot more. The Hebrew word *shalom* has a depth of meaning. I found this definition in the footnote to Psalm 34:14 in The Passion Translation: "This word means much more than peace. It means wholeness, wellness, well-being, safe, happy, friendly, favor, completeness, to make peace, peace offering, secure, to prosper, to be victorious, to be content, tranquil, quiet, and restful."

Recently, I heard someone speak of peace as universal flourishing. We all want that, and we go to lengths to get it. We want to reign over our circumstances and live victoriously over sin. So, what's the connection between coming forth in our real identity and enjoying life and peace? Let me share a few verses.

> For if, by the trespass of the one man [Adam], death reigned through that one man, how much more will those who receive God's abundant provision of grace and of the gift of righteousness **reign in life** through the one man, Jesus Christ! (Romans 5:17, emphasis added)
>
> So letting your sinful nature control your mind leads to death. But letting the Spirit control your mind leads to **life and peace**. (Romans 8:6 NLT, emphasis added)

Think back for a moment to what you read in the last chapter. For the royal you to come forth, the attachment between your soul and the Tree of Knowledge has to be broken. Your spirit has to take back its leading role under the authority of the Spirit of God. Life and peace are spirit-derived, so living from the unregenerated soul realm disconnects us from God's grace and gift of righteousness that empowers us to reign in life. Many of us speak peace affirmations from the Word of God, which is commendable. And by God's mercy, we've enjoyed dimensions of peace through the Holy Spirit. But there's more!

Isaiah 9:6-7 declares that Jesus is our Prince of Peace, that the government is on His shoulders, and of the increase of His government, there shall be no end. The reign of Jesus' government of peace must begin in our soul. As Jesus' government of peace increases, we are empowered to reign in life with Him. Isaiah 54:10 gives us a beautiful description of God's covenant of peace with us. "Though the mountains be shaken and the hills be removed, yet my unfailing love for you will not be shaken nor my covenant of peace be removed,' says the LORD, who has compassion on you."

In our royal identity, we're led by our spirit, reign in life with the Prince of Peace through God's grace and righteousness, and enjoy the blessings of God's covenant of peace.

You Operate in Spiritual Authority

You'll recall reading that we're spirit beings on an earthly journey, having bi-locational capacity. That means God has given us dominion authority in both the spiritual and natural realms. Coming forth in your royal identity causes Heaven to authorize your spiritual authority. The royal you will be recognized in both realms. Also, your authority will be respected by spiritual forces that try to oppose God's will and purposes on Earth.

Two things must be noted. First, our authority is subject to God's authority. Jesus demonstrated this submission during His earthly ministry, declaring more than once that He spoke and acted only by the Father's authority.[49] Humanity rebelled against God's sovereign authority by eating from the Tree of Knowledge. So only when our soul has come out from under the control of the Tree of Knowledge will we exercise our spiritual authority as God intended. Our royal identity positions us in Christ, and we operate in His power and authority.

What the Centurion said in Matthew 8:8-9 demonstrates the authority of our words when we are properly aligned with the authority of Heaven.

> The centurion replied, "Lord, I do not deserve to have you come under my roof. But just say the word, and my servant will be healed. For I myself am a man under authority, with soldiers under me. I tell this one, 'Go,' and he goes; and that one, 'Come,' and he comes. I say to my servant, 'Do this,' and he does it."

By the way, this is not about ordering people around. The point is that we exercise our delegated spiritual authority to accomplish God's will by our words. That's why Ecclesiastes 8:4a NKJV says, "Where the word of a king is, there is power."

Second, exercising our spiritual authority demands authenticity. But authenticity is not just being true to yourself (who you think you are). Authenticity is being true to who God created you to be. Just as we are known and recognizable in the earthly realm, the same is true in the spiritual realm. Although Satan doesn't know everything, he knows when we're not real. I believe our spiritual warfare in taking authority over evil forces will be more effective when we're operating in our royal identity and aligned with Heaven's authority.

Acts 19:13-16 records the devastating experience of the seven Sons of Sceva (a leading Jewish priest) who tried to cast out evil spirits by invoking the name of Jesus. According to the record, "They would say, "In the name of the Jesus whom Paul preaches, I command you to come out." Verses 15-16 give this report: "One day the evil spirit answered them, "Jesus I know, and Paul I know about, but who are you?" Then the man who had the evil spirit jumped on them and overpowered them all. He gave them such a beating that they ran out of the house naked and bleeding."

The problem the Sons of Sceva faced was not just that they didn't have authority over the demons they confronted. The root problem is that they confronted the demons as impostors. They were using a fake identity.

Many believers point to the experience of the Sons of Sceva as the reason to avoid spiritual warfare. The trouble with that decision is that as believers in Christ, we're on a spiritual battlefield anyway. While the proper alignment with the authority of Heaven and spiritual and earthly governmental boundaries should not be overlooked, we must recognize that our authentic royal identity carries spiritual authority.

You Pray Bold Prayers

Prayer is the believer's lifeline. Prayer is also our main service before God as a royal priesthood. (More on that in Chapter 18). Confidence in approaching God is key to having a meaningful prayer life and seeing our prayers answered. Faith isn't the only requirement for answered prayers. It requires relationship and identity revelation. Perspective and location also matter. Relocating our spiritual prayer altars to heavenly places makes a difference because we're seated there with Christ.[50] When we know the Father in a vital relationship (not just about Him) and know ourselves (who we are and how the Father sees us), we'll pray with boldness and authority.

Many times in prayer, as a prelude to the main petitions we're bringing to God, we often quote these two verses:

> Let us therefore come boldly to the throne of grace, that we may obtain mercy and find grace to help in time of need. (Hebrews 4:16 NKJV)

> The effectual fervent prayer of a righteous man availeth much. (James 5:16b KJV)

These verses boost our confidence in two ways. First, they announce that we have an invitation from God. And secondly, that we meet the criteria for getting answers to our prayers. They anchor our faith in prayer. However, unless we fully embrace our redemptive royal identity in Christ, we risk using these verses to convince God, ourselves, and others why our prayers should be answered. Also, although we may pray them loudly, it doesn't necessarily amount to the boldness and confidence that produce answered prayers.

Nevertheless, in praying the Word of God that He has given us for a particular situation, we're praying His will, which gives us confidence.[51] Bold prayers also emanate from being firmly convinced (with no hidden trace of shame or inferiority) that the blood of Jesus has reconstituted us with God's righteous DNA and identity. Second Corinthians 5:21 isn't just an affirmation; it's our constitution and baseline for praying bold prayers: "God made him who had no sin to be sin for us, so that in him we might become the righteousness of God." We've been made right with God inside and out because of Jesus and the blood of His cross. This is the truth. The Father sees us in Jesus' perfect righteousness, and we cannot allow our unregenerated souls to rob us of this confidence.

Also, we confidently pray bold prayers because they don't just benefit us and others. They advance God's Kingdom purposes as well. We listen to God's voice and release in prayer what He says. God has made us stewards of the Earth, and it's through us (as embodied spirit beings) that He has the license to operate legally on the Earth. The late Dr. Myles Munroe revealed this profound truth: "Prayer is man giving God permission or license to interfere in earth's affairs…prayer is earthly license for heavenly interference." In our royal identity, we embrace our dominion stewardship, and through prayer, we can better partner with God in bringing Heaven to Earth.

You Advance God's Kingdom Purposes

Coming forth in our royal identity enables us to see the invisible, spiritual Kingdom of God and partner with God for its advancement. We'll further explore the Kingdom dimension of our royal identity in the next chapter, but for now, let's talk about the power that comes from aligning our purpose with the purposes of God's Kingdom. Embracing our royal identity answers the first question of every human heart: Who am I? The fulfillment of our unique purpose answers the second question: Why am I here?

Queen Esther's experience exemplifies the significance of our royal identity in advancing God's Kingdom purposes. (If you aren't familiar with her story, I encourage you to read the Old Testament Book of Esther.) I'll highlight a few key points.

At the advice of her uncle, Mordecai, Esther had hidden her Jewish identity while seeking to be chosen as queen by King Xerxes of Persia. Becoming queen was a strategic plan to protect the vulnerable Jewish people throughout the region. Eventually, the time came when Esther had to come forth in her Jewish identity to save her people from annihilation. She struggled with the risk of going before the king without an invitation. Mordecai's words convinced her that she had a unique purpose to fulfill, and it was only by embracing and revealing her true identity she would fulfill that purpose.

> For if you remain silent at this time, relief and deliverance for the Jews will arise from another place, but you and your father's family will perish. And who knows but that you have come to your royal position for such a time as this? (Esther 4:14)

Like Mordecai, I'm encouraging you to embrace your royal identity because there's a unique Kingdom purpose for you to fulfill in advancing God's purposes on Earth. The wisdom and empowerment you need to fulfill that purpose are wrapped up in your royal identity.

An entire people group benefited from Queen Esther coming forth in her royal identity. Who will benefit from your coming forth? What plans of the enemy will you thwart by your coming forth? I am grateful for the grace of God that has called me forth and equipped me as a messenger of hope to the generations. Someone's breakthrough into their royal identity is dependent on your coming forth.

This quote from Rev. Dr. Martin Luther King Jr., which appeared in his letter from Birmingham, Alabama jail in 1963, greatly inspired me: "In a real sense, all life is inter-related. All men are caught in an inescapable network of mutuality, tied in a single garment of destiny. Whatever affects one directly, affects all indirectly. I can never be what I ought to be until you are what you ought to be, and you can never be what you ought to be until I am what I ought to be. This is the inter-related structure of reality."

May your coming forth in your royal identity encourage many to do likewise and serve as a catalyst for the advancement of God's kingdom purposes in your sphere of influence and beyond.

You Display God's Glory

Displaying God's glory puts you in good company with His other works of creation, as described in Psalm 19:1-6.

> The heavens declare the glory of God; the skies proclaim the work of his hands. Day after day they pour forth speech; night after night they reveal knowledge. They have no speech, they use no words; no sound is heard from them. Yet their voice goes out into all the earth, their words to the ends of the world. In the heavens God has pitched a tent for the sun. It is like a bridegroom coming out of his chamber, like a champion rejoicing to run his course. It rises at one end of the heavens and makes its circuit to the other; nothing is deprived of its warmth.

The whole creation waits for you to join this parade of God's glory. I'm fascinated that without words, their voice goes out to the ends of the Earth. There's a big encouragement here for anyone afraid of public speaking (like I was once). Your authenticity has a voice you can't afford to muzzle any longer. Daniel 12:3 says, "Those who are wise will shine like the brightness of the heavens, and those who lead many to righteousness, like the stars forever and ever."

Philippians 2:15 describes the impact of your coming forth in your royal identity: "So that you may become blameless and pure, children of God without fault in a warped and crooked generation. Then you will shine among them like stars in the sky."

The display of your glory is the light that Matthew 5:14-16 speaks about:

> You are the light of the world. A town built on a hill cannot be hidden. Neither do people light a lamp and put it under a bowl. Instead they put it on its stand, and it gives light to everyone in the house. In the same way, let your light shine before others, that they may see your good deeds and glorify your Father in heaven.

When Hebrews 2:10 speaks of Jesus bringing many sons to glory, that's not just a future reality. It's now! Your redemptive glory is for the unity of the Body of Christ and the preparation of the glorious church as the Bride of Christ.[52] It's an awesome privilege to demonstrate to the world who God is by putting His glory on display.

You Become a Generational Legacy Builder

We're each part of the great continuum of God's everlasting Kingdom. As Psalm 145:13 NKJV proclaims, "Your kingdom is an everlasting kingdom, and Your dominion endures throughout all generations." God's purposes are fulfilled generationally, so each generation has to be intentional in how it builds. Today's young generations face an unprecedented identity crisis as society becomes increasingly secularized. This reality makes the need for royal identity generational legacy builders exceptionally urgent.

Acts 13:36 says that King David served God's purposes in his generation. King David secured his legacy and ensured people had what they needed to worship God faithfully. King David couldn't build the temple for God, so he made all the necessary preparations for his son, Solomon. He gathered resources, outlined the plans, and empowered Solomon for the work.[53] Coming forth in your royal identity is one of the ways you serve God's purpose in your generation and leave a righteous identity legacy for future generations.

Each of us inherits the natural identity of the family line into which we're born. However, as you read in the section on fig leaf identities, our natural identity is not a solid foundation on which to build our self-definition. The natural identity is subject to change and imperfections.

We, therefore, must become generational legacy builders who reproduce after our redemptive royal identity. In doing so, we'll participate in God's original dominion mandate to be fruitful and multiply, not just biologically but spiritually.

In building our generational legacy, the five areas we've discussed in which Jesus accomplished the resetting of God's original design provide a framework: Being vitally connected with God as our Source, knowing God as heavenly Father, becoming reconstituted in His righteousness and glory, being established in His Kingdom, and having our soul restored to its original design under the leading of our spirit.

New and prospective parents have a unique opportunity to build this foundation in their children's lives early so they grow up with a strong sense of their God-given identity and purpose. Such generation is represented by the colt that Jesus sent His disciples to find in Luke 19:30-31— "Go to the village ahead of you, and as you enter it, you will find a colt tied there, which no one has ever ridden. Untie it and bring it here. If anyone asks you, 'Why are you untying it?' say, 'The Lord needs it.'"

My prayer and hope is that in the emerging generations, God will have a people for Himself who haven't been ensnared by identity distortions. The Master has need of them! May we, as the older generation (especially parents and grandparents), do our part to partner with Him for this cause.

I trust you've found these seven benefits of embracing and coming forth in your royal identity as motivational as they've been to me. Let me recap: Making God joyful, enjoying peace and reigning in life, operating in spiritual authority, praying bold prayers, advancing God's Kingdom purposes, displaying God's glory, and becoming a generational legacy builder.

Congratulations on reaching this milestone! You've completed the first three sections of the book. The upcoming final section is full of revelation about the royal you. Get ready for the next chapter, the book's summit— Royal Sons and Kings.

Reflection and Action

What insights did you gain from this chapter?

_____

_____

_____

_____

Specify at least two actions you'll take based on the insights gained.

1. _____

_____

2. _____

_____

SECTION FOUR

THE ROYAL YOU

CHAPTER 16

ROYAL SONS AND KINGS

There is no deep knowing of God without the deep knowing of self, and no deep knowing of self without the deep knowing of God.

— John Calvin

In this chapter, you're about to uncover a mystery concerning your royal identity in Christ that you may have overlooked because it's something you didn't know or understand. I'm referring to the mystery of being sons of God and kings—our spiritual identity, which is unrelated to biology or secular concepts. If you thought at first that the chapter title should have been "Royal Sons and Daughters," it's not an error! I didn't forget the daughters of God. Please bear with me and read on.

You've likely heard the popular sayings about the similarities between children and their parents: *Like father, like son. Like mother, like daughter.* Well, there's more to these idioms. In simple, general terms, they express the law of reproduction that God established at creation. Every living thing carries within it the seed to reproduce after its kind. Fish produce fish. Dogs produce dogs. Plants produce plants. Likewise, our Creator God, the Eternal Royal King, who is a Spirit, has produced from Himself human offspring with His Spirit essence and dominion authority.

Another principle of creation is that God created everything by speaking to a source. For each thing, He spoke to the source He wanted it to come from. For plants and animals, God spoke to the soil (Genesis 1:11, 24) so they'd have the same composition as the soil and flourish by staying connected to and receiving sustenance from the soil. Similarly, God also spoke to the water to create marine life (Genesis 1:20). For the creation of the celestial bodies, He spoke to the atmospheric gases (Genesis 1:14). However, for the creation of humanity, God spoke to Himself: "Then God said, 'Let us make man in our image, in our likeness.'" (Genesis 1:26)

To experience the glorious living you desire and deserve, you must embrace these truths about yourself: You're of the God-kind! God is the Source from which you originated, and you're at your best when connected to Him in a vital relationship.

Lookalikes of the Firstborn Royal Son

Our royal identity is the lookalike of Jesus Christ, the Firstborn Royal Son of God named King of kings and Lord of lords.[54] He is the pattern and mold from which God created humanity. Colossians 1:15 helps us to grasp the meaning and significance of being made in the image of God. "The Son is the image of the invisible God, the firstborn over all creation." You can't miss the significance of this! Christ is the image of God, and you're made in the image of God. You're, therefore, made in the image of Christ! You're an image-bearer of Christ. God made you to be like Christ, so your royal identity is in Christ.

God sees you as one created to manifest the image of God, just like Christ. You share His spiritual, intellectual, and moral attributes and are made to function like Him. That's not a small thing. Whatever ability Christ has, God has invested some of that same ability in you! First John 4:17 NKJV says, "…as He is, so are we in this world."

You are royalty like your heavenly Father and His Firstborn Royal Son, Jesus Christ!

Mysteries of Humanity's Creation

The creation blueprint of Genesis is vital to understanding our royal identity. There's an essential truth to reinforce from Chapter 2. It's in our gender-neutral spirit identity that we're royal sons and kings. God first created humanity's gender-neutral spirit (Hebrew: *'adam*) from Himself, then formed separate biological male and female bodies (Adam and Eve) to host this human spirit.

Our male and female physical bodies are essential to function in the Earth realm. According to God's creation order, spirits need a body to operate "legally" in the physical realm. (That's why God created human offspring to operate through and propagate His Kingdom. Satan and demon spirits also seek out physical bodies to operate through). As a spirit being housed in a physical body, you and I have the capacity to operate both in the spiritual and earthly realms. We are bi-locational beings. As you'll now see, the mysteries concerning our creation align with God's two predominant purposes for creating humanity.

Two Divine Purposes

A revelation of God's heart's desire and intent gives us further insight into the mysteries of humanity's creation. It also helps us answer the universal questions people grapple with, including believers: Who am I? Why am I here?

As you would have read in Chapter 2, the creation account of Genesis is only the beginning of a larger revelation unfolded in the rest of Scripture. In creation, God's heart is set on two eternal purposes. First, to be the Father to a family of human offspring like His Firstborn Son, Jesus. Second, to replicate His heavenly Kingdom in the Earth realm under the stewardship of His human offspring. Relation and dominion sum up God's eternal purposes behind creation. They explain **who** and **why** we are. As a by-product of who we are, they also help us understand **whose** we are.

Love is the Reason

God is love (1 John 4:16). Divine love is the constant motivating force behind everything God does. That means His eternal purposes of relation and dominion are love-motivated. Divine love is a Great Giver. The well-known verse of John 3:16 NKJV epitomizes Divine Love and its redemptive action. "For God so loved the world that He gave His only begotten Son, that whoever believes in Him should not perish but have everlasting life."

God's desire to give away the endless, pure love shared by the Trinity of Father, Son, and Holy Spirit motivated the Genesis creation. Above all, divine love motivated God to create us in His image and likeness because true love is reciprocated only with its kind. (The principle explains why, although Adam cared lovingly for the animals, He needed one of his kind for a reciprocal love relationship).

Let me break down this truth of God's love motivation so that your heart can receive it— *You are God's love child! You were made by love, for love, and to love. God loves you with the same love He has for Jesus.*[55]

God's love motive and eternal purposes of relation and dominion are the seedbeds of our royal identity, positioning us as sons and kings. Let's see how the Bible supports this revelation. Be prepared for the Holy Spirit to shed new light on familiar Scriptures.

Sons of God

A misunderstanding has confused God's holy desire for sons like His Firstborn. It has nothing to do with a preference for males over females. Generally speaking, the biblical principle of sonship concerns spiritual maturity to represent God the Father. This spiritual maturity doesn't depend on age, for Jesus announced at twelve that He had to be about His Father's business.[56] Remember, we're created to be sons like the Firstborn Son.

Our royal identity as sons of God is based on the spirit-image and likeness of God in which He created us. Being a royal son is defined by our gender-neutral spirit. This fundamental truth that both the male and female species of humanity posses the same gender-neutral spirit essence of God is central to our royal identity.

The many biblical references to "children of God," which we intuitively interpret through the natural lens of biological sons and daughters, sometimes eclipse this truth. Bible translations that use the expression "sons of God" are helpful. Here are some examples where the King James Version says "sons of God" instead of the politically correct expression "children of God" used in other translations.

> Behold, what manner of love the Father hath bestowed upon us, that we should be called the sons of God: therefore the world knoweth us not, because it knew him not. Beloved, now are we the sons of God, and it doth not yet appear what we shall be: but we know that, when he shall appear, we shall be like him; for we shall see him as he is. (1 John 3:1-2)

> But as many as received him, to them gave he power to become the sons of God, even to them that believe on his name: Which were born, not of blood, nor of the will of the flesh, nor of the will of man, but of God. (John 1:12-13)

It's important to pay attention to the language, bearing in mind that in some instances, earlier translations had more freedom to use language that captured the intent of God's heart.

Luke 3:38 NIV, which closes out the genealogy of Jesus with "Adam, the son of God," underscores the intent and desire of God's heart for sons like His Firstborn Son. When God created *'adam*, He created an earthly son who was, first and foremost, a spirit being. The loss of our sonship identity is an often missed consequence of the Fall of humanity. We first learned to think of the Fall of humanity in terms of spiritual death and separation from God, which is true. However, from the identity perspective, we must understand that in the Fall, Adam and Eve lost their royal identity as a spiritual son, and so did we.

When God called out to Adam and asked, "Where are you?" He held Adam (the male-man) accountable by helping him locate himself — "Where is the spirit-man *'adam* who I created?" One could say that Adam's spirit had lost its original "GPS signal." He had lost his royal sonship identity.

So, what are some defining characteristics of these royal sons that God desires?

- God desires royal sons who value and express their glorious identity of a spirit being made in the image of God and who understand that they're designed with a male or female body and a soul to function on Earth.

- God desires royal sons who live by the revelation that they're first and foremost eternal spirits engaged in an earthly human experience.

- God desires royal sons who remain attached to their Spirit Source in a vital relationship with Him as Father, Jesus as their Model, and the Holy Spirit as their supernatural Helper.

- God desires royal sons who, like Jesus, represent God's heavenly Kingdom and actively advance its presence on Earth.

These are royal sons who function as kings in dominion authority.

Kings of a Domain

"Let them have dominion" (Genesis 1:26 NKJV) expresses God's intent for the spirit man *'adam* He created to steward and represent His Kingdom on Earth. The word "dominion" signifies governance and authority and is closely associated with the concept of a kingdom or domain. This announcement of divine intent is the foundation of our royal identity as kings. Our kingship reflects God's eternal kingship and aligns with His desire for His family of human offspring to expand His dominion (kingdom rule) into the physical realm.

Being created in the image of God means we share God's identity, which includes sharing the dimension of His identity as King. Psalm 10:16 declares, for example, "The Lord is King forever and ever," and First Timothy 1:17 praises Him as King Eternal. Revelation 5:13 lauds King Jesus as the One who sits upon the throne, worthy of all glory and power forever. Created in God's image also means that we share Jesus' Kingly identity, as His title of "King of kings and Lord of lords" in Revelation 19:16 reflects.

Throughout the Old Testament, the reign of kings over Israel and Judah, beginning with King Saul, illustrates God's intent to have kings representing His Kingdom. In First Samuel 8:7, God described Israel's desire for a human king as a rejection of His rule over them as King. Nevertheless, God used their history to illustrate His intent and reveal the limitations of human authority when it is not subject to His will. King David stands out despite his shortcomings because he was a man after God's heart.[57] In his heart, he carried the revelation of God as Supreme King and ruled in submission to God's sovereign rule.

Jesus displayed and clarified many of the characteristics, principles, and standards for spiritual kings during His earthly ministry. Some significant features distinguish the Kingdom of God and our identity as kings from the world's concepts.

- The Kingdom we're part of is not of this world, but God intends that as His representatives, we will use the power and authority of His Kingdom to influence the world. In John 18:36, Jesus affirmed His kingship during His pre-crucifixion trial but clarified that His reign was spiritual. "My kingdom is not of this world."

- The Kingdom of God is the only kingdom in which all its citizens are kings. Philippians 3:20 says our citizenship is in heaven, and in Luke 22:29, Jesus said He has conferred on us a kingdom just as the Father has conferred on Him.

- Servanthood is the hallmark of the Kingdom of God, as Jesus demonstrated and explained in Matthew 20:25-28. "Jesus called them together and said, "You know that the rulers of the Gentiles lord it over them, and their high officials exercise authority over them. Not so with you. Instead, whoever wants to become great among you must be your servant, and whoever wants to be first must be your slave—just as the Son of Man did not come to be served, but to serve, and to give his life as a ransom for many."

- In our redemptive identity in Christ, we embody a merging of the dimensions of king and priest, which were separate in Old Testament times. The Bible describes us as a kingdom of priests or a royal priesthood.[58] As kings, we serve in our dominion authority; as priests, we minister to God and others.

- In our kingly authority, we're called to partner with Jesus to bring everything in the earthly realm under the government, rule, and order of God's spiritual Kingdom. Our authority to rule isn't over others but over the powers and works of darkness, as Jesus told His disciples in Luke 10:19. "I have given you authority to trample on snakes and scorpions and to overcome all the power of the enemy; nothing will harm you."

In the Fall of Adam and Eve, humanity lost its kingship authority. In His covenant with Abraham, God had promised Abraham that "kings would come from him."[59] In this covenant promise, God saw you and me, the spiritual seed of Abraham in Christ, in our royal identity as kings. Through His redemptive work of the Cross, His burial, and resurrection, Jesus has restored our capacity once again to have dominion authority on Earth and reign as kings in life.

> For if because of one man's trespass (lapse, offense) death reigned through that one, much more surely will those who receive [God's] overflowing grace (unmerited favor) and the free gift of righteousness [putting them into right standing with Himself] reign as kings in life through the one Man Jesus Christ (the Messiah, the Anointed One). (Romans 5:17 AMPC)

Our Royal Identity is a Kingdom Reality

The word "royalty" may bring images and thoughts of natural kings, queens, and monarchical government systems to mind. However, our royal identity is best understood and experienced in the context of the Kingdom of God. The dialogue between Jesus and Nicodemus in the Gospel of John confirms this truth.

Intrigued by what Jesus had been doing, Nicodemus approached Jesus with a question. He wanted to know more about what appeared to be a special kind of connection between Jesus and God. In His response, Jesus essentially said, you can have what I have and do what I do. The secret is seeing and entering the Kingdom of God!

> Jesus replied, "Very truly I tell you, no one can **see** the kingdom of God unless they are born again."
>
> "How can someone be born when they are old?" Nicodemus asked. "Surely they cannot enter a second time into their mother's womb to be born!"
>
> Jesus answered, "Very truly I tell you, no one can **enter** the kingdom of God unless they are born of water and the Spirit. Flesh gives birth to flesh, but the Spirit gives birth to spirit. (John 3:3-6, emphasis added)

I've emphasized "see" and "enter" in the above verses because they point to key dimensions of experiencing our royal identity.

When Jesus told Nicodemus he had to be born again, He identified the basic spiritual need of fallen humanity and much more. He laid down two central principles for discovering our royal identity. First, we must experience a new birth in our spirit by God's Spirit giving new life to our spirit so we can recapture the original DNA of God we had before the interruption of sin. Second, we must enter, see, and live in the realm of the Kingdom of God because our royal identity is Kingdom-based. We were created for the Kingdom of God and given authority to exercise dominion in that realm. That's why Jesus' finished work of redemption included the rescue operation and permanent migration to restore us to our original Kingdom position.

Another important principle derived from the conversation between Jesus and Nicodemus is that the dominion identity we lost in the Fall of Adam had to be redeemed and recreated. The essence of Luke 19:10 is that Jesus, the Son of Man, came to seek both "the lost" and "what" was lost. The finished work of the cross was much more than God's provision to get us to Heaven. It was to get us back to God's original relationship and Kingdom intent—"Let them have dominion!" That's the ultimate reset you read about earlier.

Here are a couple of questions to ponder.

Could it be that although believers have entered the Kingdom of God through faith in Jesus Christ, some haven't yet "seen" the Kingdom of God, so their royal identity eludes them?

Is seeing the Kingdom a missing piece of the puzzle for many who haven't yet experienced fruit from years of faithfully speaking affirmations of their identity in Christ?

A revelation of the Kingdom transcends religious forms. It's more than being a Christian or belonging to a particular brand of Christianity. While on Earth, Jesus tried to unveil the Kingdom by explaining that it is within you, among you, and has come near you. In Romans 14:17, the Apostle Paul later made the Holy Spirit connection. "For the kingdom of God is not a matter of eating and drinking, but of righteousness, peace and joy in the Holy Spirit." Let me restate the affirmative: "For the kingdom of God is righteousness, peace, and joy in the Holy Spirit."

Seeing the Kingdom comes only by the revelation of the Spirit. The revelation is so important I sense the need to sieze this moment and pray right now.

Our Glorious Father and Eternal King, for this cause, we pray that you would grant us your royal sons and kings (your beloved sons and daughters) your Spirit of wisdom and revelation to know you better so we can also know ourselves better. We ask you to enlighten the eyes of our hearts (open our spiritual eyes) to see you and your spiritual Kingdom like never before. By your Holy Spirit, may we experience the power of your Kingdom at work in us — the righteousness of Christ, His peace (universal flourishing), and the joy of celebrating who we are in Him. We pray with thanksgiving and in the authority of the Name of Jesus. Amen.

Identity Lost and Found

By understanding the desire of God's heart for royal spiritual sons, we develop lenses to see hidden kernels in many things Jesus said and did during His earthly ministry. His parable of the lost son in Luke 15:11-31 is perhaps one of the most revealing accounts of the loss and restoration of our royal identity.

The father in the story demonstrates our heavenly Father's heart of love in restoring us to our positions of sonship, relationship, and dominion even after we've made a mess of things. Upon his return, the son who had left his father's house and wasted his inheritance was laden with guilt, shame, and condemnation. He had settled for the identity of a servant and wanted his father's buy-in, but His father would have none of it!

> The son said to him, 'Father, I have sinned against heaven and against you. I am no longer worthy to be called your son.' But the father said to his servants, 'Quick! Bring the best robe and put it on him. Put a ring on his finger and sandals on his feet. Bring the fattened calf and kill it. Let's have a feast and celebrate. For this son of mine was dead and is alive again; he was lost and is found.' So they began to celebrate. (Luke 15:21-24)

The robe replaced the fig leaf identity of a slave the son had adopted. His father clothed him in a royal robe symbolic of Jesus' robe of righteousness, far superior to the fig leaves Adam and Eve tried to cover themselves with, even the animal skin God used to cover them. The ring symbolized dominion authority, enabling him to transact business on behalf of his father. The sandals confirmed the restoration of his status as a son because only slaves went barefooted. Killing the fattened calf was for the blood, not just the meat. Like the slain animal in Eden whose skin covered Adam and Eve, the fattened calf was yet another foreshadowing of Jesus' crucifixion and the shedding of His redemptive blood for our restoration to God's original intent. Finally, this parable shows how much the Father rejoices when we are restored to our royal identity.

The complaining older son who remained at home is a stark awakening that it is possible to be active in the Father's house (engrossed in church service) and still not know the love of our heavenly Father or our royal identity as a son and king.[60] Like the younger son, he was also outside the Romans 14:17 realm of the Kingdom. His righteousness (being in the right standing with his father) was performance-based. He had no peace (could not flourish) because he didn't know his father's heart of love for him. He also had no joy, so instead of celebrating, he complained. He had made servanthood his identity instead of sonship.

I'll close this chapter with a profound identity proclamation from Pastor Bill and the late Beni Johnson of Bethel in Redding, California, that sums up and clarifies the various dimensions of our royal identity.

"Royalty is my identity. Servanthood is my assignment. Intimacy with God is my life Source. So before God, I'm an intimate. Before people I'm a servant. Before the powers of hell I'm a ruler, with no tolerance for their influence. Wisdom knows which role to fulfill at the proper time."[61]

In the next chapter, we'll explore the dimension of servanthood.

Reflection and Action

What insights did you gain from this chapter?

_____

_____

_____

_____

Specify at least two actions you'll take based on the insights gained.

1. _____

   _____

2. _____

   _____

CHAPTER 17

SERVANT LEADERS

*Holy Spirit, shape my heart.
Knock off any rough areas of insecurity.
Seal up the truth of my identity in my heart
so I can serve like Jesus did.*

— *Bill & Beni Johnson*

Servanthood is not our identity. It is our assignment as royal sons and kings. More precisely, servanthood is the heart attitude that motivates whatever we do to serve God, His Church, Kingdom, and people. Jesus epitomizes servanthood. His actions and words set the ultimate example of a servant leader. His top mission in coming to Earth was to pour out His life for humanity to be restored to the Father for His two eternal purposes: relationship and dominion. Everything Jesus did was for this royal service, ultimately offering His life and blood for our redemption by dying on the cross.

Jesus demonstrated servanthood in His day-to-day ministry on Earth, from healing the sick to raising the dead to washing His disciples' feet. His words unequivocally revealed that servanthood is the highest standard for the Kingdom of God and its citizens.

> But Jesus called them together and said, "You know that the rulers in this world lord it over their people, and officials flaunt their authority over those under them. But among you it will be different. Whoever wants to be a leader among you must be your servant, and whoever wants to be first among you must become your slave. For even the Son of Man came not to be served but to serve others and to give his life as a ransom for many." (Matthew 20:25-28 NLT)

In contrast to the world, greatness in the Kingdom is defined by serving rather than by power and authority. Leaders in the Kingdom are servant leaders, valuing the worth of others and not thinking of any job too low for them to do, even washing the feet of others as Jesus did.

> After washing their feet, he put on his robe again and sat down and asked, "Do you understand what I was doing? You call me 'Teacher' and 'Lord,' and you are right, because that's what I am. And since I, your Lord and Teacher, have washed your feet, you ought to wash each other's feet. I have given you an example to follow. Do as I have done to you. I tell you the truth, slaves are not greater than their master. Nor is the messenger more important than the one who sends the message. Now that you know these things, God will bless you for doing them. (John 13:12-17 NLT)

Do you cringe when you read the words servant and slave in these passages? I once had someone leave a session because she found the words obnoxious. I understood her point of view. It seems contradictory on the surface and in the natural. How can a royal son be a servant? And who has ever heard of a servant king? Let's put these words into perspective.

The Concepts of Servants and Slaves

Jesus' example and teaching about servant leadership usually generate two different responses. On the one hand, servants and slaves strike a negative chord because of their association with historical and cultural experiences. On the other hand, with noble intentions, some plunge unreservedly into doing various service works. The desire is to be useful to the Lord by practicing what Jesus taught and modeled.

However, both responses miss the mark. Based on the Greek word *doulos*, translated as servant and slave, the biblical concept means a voluntary, spiritual submission to the authority and will of a loving and righteous God. The Apostle Paul, a Roman Citizen, affirms this in Romans 1:1 by referring to himself as a slave or bondslave of Jesus Christ and a chosen apostle. Although a free man, Paul chose complete dependence and obedience to Jesus Christ.

The elements of brutality and dehumanization associated with oppressive systems of slavery have no place in the biblical concept of servant leadership. Also, when we engage in extensive works of service without the proper identity foundation, we end up unwittingly being controlled and defined by our work. Let's look at what may not be obvious in Jesus' example of servanthood.

Jesus Served as a Son

There's a critical truth about Jesus' model of servanthood that we must not miss. Jesus served from His identity as the beloved Son of His heavenly Father. His relationship with His Father defined Him, not His service. In other words, Jesus served *from* identity, not *for* identity. Unless we're secure in our royal identity as spiritual sons of God, we risk using our acts of service to consciously or subconsciously define ourselves. When that happens, we're left with nothing more than a performance-based fig leaf identity.

Philippians 2:5-8 is regarded as the believer's code of humility and servanthood.

> You must have **the same attitude that Christ Jesus had**. Though he was God, he did not think of equality with God as something to cling to. Instead, **he gave up his divine privileges**; he took the humble position of a slave and was born as a human being. When he appeared in human form, he humbled himself in obedience to God and died a criminal's death on a cross. (NLT, emphasis added)

I intentionally used the New Living Translation for a couple of reasons. Verse five reinforces the earlier point that servanthood is a heart attitude of lovingly and humbly serving God and others. Also, the language of verse seven highlights that what Jesus gave up was His "divine privileges." In coming to the Earth as a human, Jesus did not cling to the glory He possessed as part of the Godhead or the privilege of operating in His inherent power and authority as God. He subjected Himself to human limitations (except that He knew no sin).

Here's the key. The one thing Jesus clung to as a man was His identity as a beloved Son—the Firstborn Royal Son of His heavenly Father. What transpired at Jesus' baptism before the start of His earthly ministry is highly significant. Let's read Matthew's account:

> When He had been baptized, Jesus came up immediately from the water; and behold, the heavens were opened to Him, and He saw the Spirit of God descending like a dove and alighting upon Him. And suddenly a voice came from heaven, saying, "This is My beloved Son, in whom I am well pleased." (Matthew 3:16 NKJV)

We can't miss the three significant happenings at Jesus' baptism: the heavens opened, the Holy Spirit descended and sat upon Jesus, and the Father affirmed His identity. The New Living Translation of the affirmation is beautiful: "This is my dearly loved Son, who brings me great joy."

If Jesus, the Son of God, needed encounters like this to launch Him into service officially, you'll agree that we need it even more. After all, He is our ultimate example and model of servanthood. When we receive Christ and are water baptized, our leaders and others may think we're ready for service, but not so fast. Wouldn't the encounters of an open heaven, the presence (empowerment) of the Holy Spirit, and the heavenly Father's blessing on our sonship identity launch us off on the right footing as servant leaders? Could it be that when these are missing, we risk the danger of performing *for* identity rather than *from* identity?

The Father's blessing of our identity is not meant to be a one-time experience either. We don't know how often Jesus may have received identity affirmations during His private prayer times. However, the Father again openly affirmed Jesus' sonship at another pivotal juncture in His ministry. Jesus was on a mountain with Peter, James, and John when His appearance was transformed with His face and clothing shining brilliantly. Seeing Jesus' transfiguration and the appearance of Moses and Elijah, Peter suggested that they memorialize the moment with three physical tabernacles.

The Father intercepted Peter's idea. Matthew 17:5 NLT says, "But even as he spoke, a bright cloud overshadowed them, and a voice from the cloud said, "This is my dearly loved Son, who brings me great joy. Listen to him." The Father's instruction to listen to Jesus emphasized the need to pay close attention to whatever Jesus says and not be distracted by other "voices." God's instruction reminds me of the question He asked Adam in the Garden: "Who told you that you were naked?" (Genesis 3:11a)

As God used this question to help Adam locate Himself and be aware of the voice that had influenced him, we also need similar awareness. When it comes to our Christian service, we must be aware that if we're not listening to the voice of sonship, we'll fall prey to voices that echo the Tree of Knowledge of Good and Evil. These counterfeit voices will plunge us into the deception of self-service under the guise of serving God or working for Him.

According to Galatians 4:6, we have the indwelling Spirit of Sonship. "Because you are his sons, God sent the Spirit of his Son into our hearts, the Spirit who calls out, *"Abba*, Father."" May we align with, hear, and echo this voice of the Spirit.

The Abuse of Work

Work is fundamental to fulfilling the dominion mandate God gave humanity at creation. Genesis 2:15 says, "The LORD God took the man and put him in the Garden of Eden to work it and take care of it." Our present-day Garden of Eden is our homes, the marketplace, the community, and the Kingdom. As New Testament believers, in the context of our church community and the Kingdom, we serve in various capacities to meet practical and spiritual needs.

We follow Jesus' example in working just as He followed the Father's. In John 5, Jesus explains:

> My Father is always at his work to this very day, and I too am working...Very truly I tell you, the Son can do nothing by himself; he can do only what he sees his Father doing, because whatever the Father does the Son also does. For the Father loves the Son and shows him all he does. Yes, and he will show him even greater works than these, so that you will be amazed. (John 5:17b, 19-20)

It is not unusual for works of service to be part of the written or unwritten code of behavior in many church communities. However, works of service can be abused when sonship is not taught, understood, or prioritized. The late Dr. Myles Munroe left us a brilliant principle that can be applied to our works of service: "When the purpose of a thing is not known, abuse is inevitable."

You may be wondering how it applies. Gaining our identity from what we do is an abuse of work. Likewise, in church circles, evaluating a person's significance, value, and worth by service is also an abuse of servanthood. It's possible to develop an unhealthy relationship with work when we call ourselves "servants of God" without first being established in our identity as sons. Subconsciously, we may depend on our work to give us a sense of right standing with God (righteousness). But that's settling for works-based righteousness instead of receiving by faith God's gift of righteousness that's ours in Christ Jesus.

In the Bible, God called or appointed many people as His servants, including Abraham, Moses, Isaiah, Cyrus, and Jesus.[62] He also identified Israel, an entire people group, as His servant.[63] The concept applies to obeying God's will and accomplishing His purpose. It's an honor to be called a servant of God. We must nevertheless recognize that servant of God is an honorary title that points to what one does, not who they are intrinsically. So, even the servant leader expression is a descriptive title, not an identity definition.

It's noteworthy that although Jesus modeled servanthood for His disciples and encouraged them to serve, He promoted them from servants to friends based on the criteria of following His command.

> You are my friends if you do what I command. I no longer call you servants, because a servant does not know his master's business. Instead, I have called you friends, for everything that I learned from my Father I have made known to you. (John 15:14-15)

What does this mean? In our royal identity, we are sons and kings who serve as servant leaders and friends of God.

Characteristics of Servant Leaders

From Jesus' parable of the two sons in Luke 15, His other teachings, and His life examples, let's summarize some key characteristics of servant leaders who are established in their royal identity as sons and kings. It will be helpful for our next chapter — On Kingdom Assignment.

As servant leaders . . .

- We lead by serving *from* identity, not *for* identity. As sons, we're about our heavenly Father's business, even as Jesus did at twelve when He stayed behind in the temple.[64]

- We do not perform for God's acceptance or the approval of others. We know we're already accepted in the Beloved.[65] Our security isn't defined by what others think or say about us, only by our heavenly Father's unfailing love.

- We're deeply rooted in our relationship with God, trusting and relying on our heavenly Father's heart of love and voluntarily submitting to His will and authority.

- We operate in the opposite spirit of the Tree of Knowledge of Good and Evil that promotes self-will, independence, and pride. We're continually releasing ourselves from the Tree of Knowledge and reattaching ourselves to the Tree of Life as our Source.

- Serving is not about what we can do for God but what God can do through us.

- As servant kings, we do not seek power. Rather, we seek the growth, well-being, and spiritual maturity of others. Our leadership uplifts and empowers others. Our value system is the opposite of the world's, measuring greatness by humility, love, and service to others rather than our power and control.

- We use our power and authority in alignment with the Father's will to advance the Kingdom and for the benefit of others.

An Open Invitation From Jesus

In closing this chapter, let me share an open invitation from Jesus. It's from the Message Bible paraphrase of Matthew 11:28-30—"Are you tired? Worn out? Burned out on religion? Come to me. Get away with me and you'll recover your life. I'll show you how to take a real rest. Walk with me and work with me—watch how I do it. Learn the unforced rhythms of grace. I won't lay anything heavy or ill-fitting on you. Keep company with me and you'll learn to live freely and lightly."

Coming forth in your royal identity may require a resetting of your servanthood. At first, it may be awkward or difficult to say "no" if you've been accustomed to saying "yes" to everything and everyone. You may have even convinced yourself that the work will never get done unless you do it. The key is to deepen your relationship with the Father to see what He's doing and do what He does, to work where He's working. May the Holy Spirit teach us the unforced rhythms of grace so that our servanthood will honor God and advance His Kingdom.

Reflection and Action

What insights did you gain from this chapter?

_____

_____

_____

_____

Specify at least two actions you'll take based on the insights gained.

1. _____

_____

2. _____

_____

CHAPTER 18

ON KINGDOM ASSIGNMENT

*But the people who know their God will prove
themselves strong and shall stand firm and do exploits [for God].*

— Daniel 11:32b AMPC

What on Earth Am I Here For? In 2002, a book published by Pastor Rick Warren of Saddleback Church with this sub-title profoundly impacted the world. With its focus on living purposefully to find meaning in life, *The Purpose Driven Life* appealed to a universal human need. The book crossed religious boundaries and resonated with people from all walks of life. Its central message was clear—life isn't about self-fulfillment but living for something bigger than ourselves by aligning with God's purpose.

Who we are and why we're here are closely connected, so our alignment with God's purpose will follow when we discover and embrace our royal identity. In the previous two chapters, we tackled the question, Who am I? This chapter will explore the second universal question: Why am I here?

Discovering My Why

The timing of the publication of *The Purpose Driven Life* was perfect. Having just encountered God's divine call (in the message "It's time to see yourself the way you really are"), I was ready to do what God had placed me on Earth to do. However, in the formative years of coming into my royal identity, my eagerness to serve God's purpose almost became a snare. I thought I was on the right path as long as I was busily engaged in church service. My thinking had to be changed.

The Holy Spirit worked through different situations to transform my mind. First, by using Matthew 7:21-23, the Lord made me aware of the need to discern and be intentional in doing His assignment. I realized this passage wasn't only a safeguard against performing Kingdom-related services in the name of Jesus without a true commitment to Him. It was also a safeguard against engaging in services He didn't assign me to do.

> Not everyone who says to Me, 'Lord, Lord,' shall enter the kingdom of heaven, but he who does the will of My Father in heaven. Many will say to Me in that day, 'Lord, Lord, have we not prophesied in Your name, cast out demons in Your name, and done many wonders in Your name?' And then I will declare to them, 'I never knew you; depart from Me, you who practice lawlessness!' (NKJV)

The language of the 2003 Bible edition I was using at the time put the fear of God (reverential awe for loyalty to God) in my heart. Verse 23b said, "The things you did were unauthorized." The words of the Apostle Paul in First Corinthians 3:12-15 reinforced the alert. I needed to safeguard against my well-intentioned works being tested by God and burned for wrong motives or other reasons.

> Now if anyone builds on this foundation with gold, silver, precious stones, wood, hay, straw, each one's work will become clear; for the Day will declare it, because it will be revealed by fire; and the fire will test each one's work, of what sort it is. If anyone's work which he has built on it endures, he will receive a reward. If anyone's work is burned, he will suffer loss; but he himself will be saved, yet so as through fire. (NKJV)

The second wave of transformation came through a theology course. In speaking about believers being God's garden producing spiritual fruit to satisfy Him, the professor asked, What fruit are you bringing the Lord?[66] His follow-up brought an awakening. He announced that God created each of us to produce one big, unique fruit. It's the expression of God's glory in and through us that only we can bring forth. This fruit isn't measured by size but by significance in God's eyes. However, as he emphasized, many believers are bringing the Lord many small fruits (gleanings), hoping they will amount to something big that satisfies the Lord. His closure was definite: It doesn't!

The third experience was a divine instruction I kept receiving while reading the Gospel of John: Watch what Jesus does! I'll elaborate momentarily. Before I do, let me say that sharing my experiences is not a license for anyone to fold their hands or neglect serving in the church. Rather, let it encourage you to seek the Lord's discernment for revelation on what is your unique why. The Bible advocates doing whatever your hands find to do. The grace of God wastes nothing. The truth is that many of us will discover our unique purpose from the works of service we engage in. The secret is to avoid the snare of a performance identity as a substitute for discovering and fulfilling your unique kingdom assignment.

Watch What Jesus Does

(I just wrote those words and realized they're a variation of the WWJD acronym for What Would Jesus Do?!)

Apart from Jesus' heart-attitude of serving God and others discussed in the last chapter, I'll identify three dimensions of Jesus' ministry in the Gospel of John that caught my attention: Jesus was clear and unwavering about His Kingdom assignment, He prioritized relationships, and His work was rooted in prayer. (I'm sure there are more in all four Gospels).

Concerning His assignment, Jesus gave a blanket declaration of His mission in John 6:38—"For I have come down from heaven not to do my will but to do the will of him who sent me." Jesus came to Earth on a redemptive mission with many dimensions and expressions. He came to restore God's spiritual Kingdom presence and authority on Earth by destroying the devil's works and restoring humanity to God's original intent.

Jesus made His Kingly identity and purpose known in His pre-crucifixion trial.

> Jesus answered, "My kingdom is not of this world. If My kingdom were of this world, My servants would fight, so that I should not be delivered to the Jews; but now My kingdom is not from here." Pilate therefore said to Him, "Are You a king then?" Jesus answered, "You say rightly that I am a king. **For this cause I was born, and for this cause I have come into the world,** that I should bear witness to the truth. Everyone who is of the truth hears My voice." (John 18:36-37 NKJV, emphasis added)

Jesus fulfilled the purpose for which He was born by surrendering fully to the Father's will, although it meant going the way of the cross. Hebrews 12:2 speaks of the joy set before Jesus. It encourages us to fix our eyes on Him to have the same endurance in fulfilling our Kingdom assignment: "Fixing our eyes on Jesus, the pioneer and perfecter of faith. For the joy set before him he endured the cross, scorning its shame, and sat down at the right hand of the throne of God."

The second dimension is that Jesus' relationship with His heavenly Father was the Source of everything He did and the hallmark of His life. He lived as one with His Father, demonstrating that it was the way we were designed to live and work. Jesus' oneness with the Father was such a novel idea that it offended the religious leaders of His time. They wanted to kill Him for claiming that God was His Father.[67]

Jesus' relationship and partnership with the Father reflected the unity and relationship of the Divine Trinity of Father, Son, and Holy Spirit. Creation was a divine partnership as the language of Genesis 1:26 NKJV confirms, "Let Us make man in Our image, according to Our likeness." The Holy Spirit hovered and brooded. The Son, Jesus the Word, was the power by which all things were created.[68] In personifying Jesus as Wisdom, Proverbs 8:30-31 describes Jesus as a craftsman working alongside the Father: "Then I was constantly at his side. I was filled with delight day after day, rejoicing always in his presence, rejoicing in his whole world and delighting in mankind." The Father also desires partnership with us as His sons.

Jesus also chose twelve disciples to partner with Him in the ministry work.[69] In doing so, Jesus demonstrated that we also need a partnership with others to fulfill God's purpose. Besides their training, the assignments, and the authority Jesus delegated to His disciples, Mark's gospel identifies a unique relational purpose. Mark 3:14a says, "He appointed twelve that they might be with him." Just as Jesus' relationship with the Father and

His disciples was vital to the success of His Kingdom assignment, we must also invest in our relationship with God and others.

Thirdly, I saw that Jesus' work was fully rooted in prayer. Jesus started His ministry with prayer and fasting in the wilderness.[70] Luke 6:12-13 also inserts prayer as a precursor to choosing His twelve disciples. "One of those days Jesus went out to a mountainside to pray, and spent the night praying to God. When morning came, he called his disciples to him and chose twelve of them, whom he also designated apostles." In many other instances, we read of Jesus retreating to pray in solitude. These special times of intimate prayer fellowship with the Father were usually early in the morning or after ministering to the multitudes.

In a sense, we could say that Jesus received His daily work orders from the Father. While in prayer, Jesus heard what the Father said and saw what He did. He'd then bring Heaven to Earth through His words and actions.

> Jesus gave them this answer: "Very truly I tell you, the Son can do nothing by himself; he can do only what he sees his Father doing, because whatever the Father does the Son also does. For the Father loves the Son and shows him all he does. Yes, and he will show him even greater works than these, so that you will be amazed. (John 5:19-20)

> For I did not speak on my own, but the Father who sent me commanded me to say all that I have spoken. I know that his command leads to eternal life. So whatever I say is just what the Father has told me to say." (John 12:49-50)

> Don't you believe that I am in the Father, and that the Father is in me? The words I say to you I do not speak on my own authority. Rather, it is the Father, living in me, who is doing his work. (John 14:10)

Maintaining a vital connection with our heavenly Father as our Source through prayer is indispensable for completing our Kingdom assignment. We need to open our ears morning by morning as one being taught. We need to listen and heed His commands. The indwelling Holy Spirit, who knows the thoughts and intents of God's heart, will reveal them to us.[71]

Your Why is Unique to You

Jesus' Kingdom assignment preceded Him. The same is true for you. Your Kingdom assignment is yours to discover, not to create. Your why is in you! That's a profound truth to internalize. You came to this Earth with a piece of eternity in your heart that's unique to you. With your cooperation, God will make it beautiful in its time. What God told Jeremiah is true of you. He knew you before you were born and appointed you for a special purpose. Even more, He designed you to fit your purpose. God has reset everything about you in your royal identity. You're synchronized with the cadence of a beautiful poetic composition.

> He has made everything beautiful in its time. He has also set eternity in the human heart; yet no one can fathom what God has done from beginning to end. (Ecclesiastes 3:11)
>
> Before I formed you in the womb I knew you, before you were born I set you apart; I appointed you as a prophet to the nations." (Jeremiah 1:5)
>
> We have become his poetry, a re-created people that will fulfill the destiny he has given each of us, for we are joined to Jesus, the Anointed One. Even before we were born, God planned in advance our destiny and the good works we would do to fulfill it! (Ephesians 2:10 TPT)

Your unique Kingdom assignment is your unique glory. Christ has entrusted dimensions of Himself to you that only you can express. Christ is in you as your hope of glory, as Colossians 1:27 says. All creation is waiting for your glory to be revealed. God is also waiting for the manifestation of your glory. It is part of the mysterious elements that will bring forth the reality of the unity of the Body of Christ according to John 17:22 – "I have given them the glory that you gave me, that they may be one as we are one."

It's also important to know that being created as a biological male or female is part of your unique glory. As royal sons and kings, we're all created in the image of God with the same gender-neutral spirit. God was purposeful, however, in designing us with gender-specific bodies for functionality. How we fulfill our Kingdom assignments and roles differs for males and females. Still, we're equally valuable and designed to be complementary.[72]

In fulfilling your Kingdom assignment, you must be aware of non-negotiable prerequisites. As it is in the marketplace, organizations often include prerequisites in their postings for job vacancies. Although your Kingdom assignment is unique to you with no competing applicants, there's an analogy regarding prerequisites. Your royal identity is Kingdom-based, and as the name implies, so is your Kingdom assignment. As God told Nicodemus, we must experience new spiritual birth by the Spirit of God to enter the Kingdom of God. Not only must we enter the Kingdom, but we must also see and live in its reality. We must prioritize the Kingdom as Jesus said in Matthew 6:33 — "But seek first his kingdom and his righteousness, and all these things will be given to you as well." (God supplies the material necessities of life as we prioritize His Kingdom and righteousness).

Developing a dominion mindset (mental attitude) is essential for fulfilling your Kingdom assignment. That's because our beliefs are the most important factor in determining what we accomplish in life. The foundation of a dominion mindset is the revelation of God's intent to extend His heavenly Kingdom to the Earth and our alignment with God's agenda. With a dominion mindset, we embrace our heavenly citizenship and royal identity as spiritual sons and kings with authority and power to accomplish God's purposes. We bring our perspectives and thinking into agreement with the principles and values of the Kingdom of God.

Having a dominion mindset isn't automatic. It's part of the transformation process we undergo in coming forth in our royal identity. (More on that in Chapter 19). According to Jesus' parable of the wineskins,[73] developing a dominion mindset is equivalent to becoming new wineskins with the capacity to operate beyond the confines of a particular brand of Christianity.

Our Kingdom assignment is multifaceted. We'll dedicate the remainder of this chapter to exploring certain aspects: Serving as a royal priesthood, embracing our kingly authority, and our deployment as royal ambassadors everywhere.

Serving as a Royal Priesthood

The identity affirmation of being a royal priesthood is well-known among many born-again believers. It's spoken from the pulpit, in prayer, and we also speak it to empower ourselves and others. It's important to know what the Scripture says and equally important to know how to fulfill it. We'll highlight the anchor verses and discuss how we serve in this capacity.

> But you are a chosen people, a royal priesthood, a holy nation, God's special possession, that you may declare the praises of him who called you out of darkness into his wonderful light. (1 Peter 2:9)

> And from Jesus Christ, the faithful witness, the firstborn from the dead, and the ruler over the kings of the earth. To Him who loved us and washed us from our sins in His own blood, and has made us kings and priests to His God and Father, to Him be glory and dominion forever and ever. Amen. (Revelation 1:5-6 NKJV)

> And they sang a new song, saying: "You are worthy to take the scroll, and to open its seals; for You were slain, and have redeemed us to God by Your blood out of every tribe and tongue and people and nation, and have made us kings and priests to our God; and we shall reign on the earth." (Revelation 5:9-10 NKJV)

We can't read those verses from Revelation and not realize that the redemption of our priesthood is part of the ultimate reset Jesus accomplished through the blood of His cross. In Exodus 28-29 and most of the Book of Leviticus, we have extensive details on the priesthood requirements for Aaron and His sons, including their clothing, preparation, consecration, and sacrifices. The presence of sin shaped this priestly order and its requirements. By offering His lifeblood to God once and for all, Jesus fulfilled the extensive sacrificial offerings that were part of the Aaronic Priestly Order. Nevertheless, the extensive details alert us to the significance of the priestly service as a reflection of God's intent for humanity and His holiness.

All believers participate in the service of a royal priesthood through Jesus, so understanding His High Priestly calling will help us understand our priestly service. Jesus did not belong to the Aaronic (Levitical) order of priests. The Father established Him (and us) in a higher eternal priestly order, which the Bible calls the Order of Melchizedek.

We first read about Melchizedek in Genesis 14:18-20 when Abraham met him after defeating enemy kings and rescuing his nephew, Lot. He was not a normal human being, as Hebrews 7:1-3 tells us:

> This Melchizedek was king of Salem and priest of God Most High. He met Abraham returning from the defeat of the kings and blessed him, and Abraham gave him a tenth

> of everything. First, the name Melchizedek means "king of righteousness"; then also, "king of Salem" means "king of peace." Without father or mother, without genealogy, without beginning of days or end of life, resembling the Son of God, he remains a priest forever.

Bible scholars have described Melchizedek as a pre-incarnate Christ. Did you notice that this king-priest has no natural lineage? That's significant. Exalting our ancestry above our divine lineage in Christ will compromise our service as a royal priesthood. Quoting Psalm 2:7 and Psalm 110:4, the writer of Hebrews declares something noteworthy. As it was for Jesus, let the Father first affirm our sonship identity so we can operate in the Melchizedek Priestly Order.

> In the same way, Christ did not take on himself the glory of becoming a high priest. But God said to him, "You are my Son; today I have become your Father." And he says in another place, "You are a priest forever, in the order of Melchizedek." (Hebrews 5:5-6)

So, how do we serve as New Testament priests after the Order of Melchizedek?

- Being of this eternal order, we have the privilege of serving as both kings and priests (which was not allowed under the Aaronic Order). In a moment, we'll talk about exercising our kingly authority. Please take note, for now, that exercising our kingly authority hinges on embracing our sonship and the higher Priestly Order of Melchizedek. We hardly hear much spoken about this Priestly Order, so it's either overlooked or misunderstood. In Hebrews 5:11, the Apostle Paul acknowledged that it was hard to explain this mystery because the people lacked spiritual capacity. Ask the Holy Spirit to give you the revelation of this New Testament Priestly Order to which you belong.

- We minister to God and offer spiritual sacrifices to declare His glory. The first spiritual sacrifice we offer God is the presentation of our bodies as a living sacrifice, holy and acceptable to God. We dedicate our entire being and everything we do to God in worship. Our spiritual sacrifices also include praise, thanksgiving, and acts of goodwill to others. (Deuteronomy 21:5, 1 Peter 2:5,9, Romans 12:1, Hebrews 13:15-16)

- Our service as a royal priesthood includes intercession (as a go-between) on behalf of others. With our priestly identity rooted in Christ, we have boldness in coming before God because Jesus has interceded for us so that we can also intercede for others. The Holy Spirit also helps our intercession. (Hebrews 4:14-16, 7:25, Romans 8:26-27)

- In addition to praying for others, we also speak words of blessing over them in the name of the Lord. (Deuteronomy 21:5, Numbers 6:22-27)

- We must wear the spiritual garment of Jesus' righteousness to ensure we're not disqualified in the spirit realm. What we're wearing determines our authority in the spiritual realm. Although Joshua, the high priest, was an Old Testament priest, the principle of Satan accusing him remains applicable. Zechariah 3 gives the account of God changing Joshua's clothing and turban so he could function effectively and stand before His courts to make righteous judgments.

- We must also guard our hearts against pride, rebellion, unbelief, and other conditions associated with the Tree of Knowledge and our unregenerated soul. (Proverbs 4:23, 1 Samuel 16:7)

Exercising Our Kingly Authority

In our royal identity, we are priests AND kings! These two functions are fluid. They feed and impact each other. It's not one or the other. It's both. When we understand and embrace our function as a royal priesthood after the Order of Melchizedek, we'll be better equipped and more inclined to exercise our kingly authority. As spiritual kings of the domain God has entrusted to us, we have the responsibility to partner with Him to see Isaiah 9:6-7a NKJV fulfilled: "For to us a Child is born, unto us a Son is given; and the government will be upon His shoulder… Of the increase of His government and peace there will be no end."

We exercise our kingly authority in prayer by hearing what God says and declaring it on the Earth. Ecclesiastes 8:4 NKJV says, "Where the word of a king is, there is power; and who may say to him, "What are you doing?" What we set in place through our kingly decrees results from what has transpired in our priestly function.

The belief among many believers that intercession is only for special believers is a lie of Satan that has severely weakened the church. You now understand that as a royal priesthood, you don't only pray for yourself and matters that concern you. This wrong belief has not only sabotaged our capacity to reign as kings on Earth. It has prevented us from partnering effectively with God to fulfill our original dominion mandate and advance God's Kingdom on Earth. Revelation 5:10 NKJV tells us explicitly, "And have made us kings and priests to our God; and we shall reign on the earth."

We've seen the languishing of the prayer ministry in many churches because of this wrong belief. Similarly, it has caused many Christians to adopt a passive attitude towards the works of Satan. I've often thought about how the Fall of humanity would have been averted if Adam and Eve had exercised their authority over the serpent. They had it, according to Genesis 1:26. They just didn't use it. Jesus overcame Satan in the wilderness with the Word of God. We also have the Word, and we have Jesus' victorious blood.

> And they overcame him by the blood of the Lamb and by the word of their testimony, and they did not love their lives to the death. (Revelation 12:11 NKJV)

Let's increase our fellowship with the blood and the Word so we can use them as the formidable weapons they are. Do you fellowship with the blood daily through the Holy Communion? (More on the Holy Communion in the next chapter). Are you aware of what the Word of God says the blood of Jesus has done for you? Are you speaking it forth? And finally, to what extent are you prepared to bring your soul life to the cross so it operates under the authority of your regenerated spirit?

While the principle of jurisdictional and territorial authority cannot be ignored, believers need not fear becoming what one author has called needless casualties of war. Remember the key. Exercising our kingly authority does not stand on its own. It flows out of our priestly ministry. We hear what God says; we see what He does, and we do likewise in proper alignment with jurisdictional apostolic authority over regions and territories.

Deployed as Royal Ambassadors Everywhere

Jesus Christ accomplished the ultimate reconciliation through the blood of His cross. In our Kingdom assignment, we're called to be His ambassadors of reconciliation.

> All this is from God, who reconciled us to himself through Christ and gave us the ministry of reconciliation: that God was reconciling the world to himself in Christ, not counting people's sins against them. And he has committed to us the message of reconciliation. We are therefore Christ's ambassadors, as though God were making his appeal through us. We implore you on Christ's behalf: Be reconciled to God. (2 Corinthians 5:18-20)

Evangelism has been and will always be part of our Kingdom assignment to rescue souls from the dominion of darkness and partner with Jesus in their migration into the Kingdom of God. Influencing the major spheres[74] of culture with the principles, values, and ethics of the Kingdom of God is also a critical part of what it means to disciple nations. With the help of Kingdom leaders like Dr. Ed Silvoso, founder of the Transform Our World Network, we understand that the Commissions recorded in Mark 16:15-18 and Matthew 28:19-20 have a different focus. While Mark has an individual mandate (evangelism), Matthew's mandate is corporate (to disciple and baptize nations and people groups for God's Kingdom culture to prevail among them).[75]

In fulfilling our Kingdom assignment, we must be prepared to bring the influence of the Kingdom into every sphere of culture. I had the privilege this past year to collaborate with Chaplain Dr. Dudley Mayers on the publication of his book *Kingdom Chaplains Everywhere: Advancing Spiritual Care and Cultural Transformation*.[76] The Kingdom Brand of Chaplaincy is God's optimal deployment strategy whereby we can be engaged as ambassadors of reconciliation everywhere, beginning in our families.

Deuteronomy 21:5 contains a dimension of our royal priestly service that we must be intentional about. "Then the Levitical priests must step forward, for the LORD your God has chosen them to minister before him and to **pronounce blessings in the LORD's name**. They are to decide all legal and criminal cases." (NLT, emphasis added) Melchizedek spoke a blessing over Abraham, God prescribed a blessing for the Aaronic priesthood to speak over the people, and Jesus spoke blessings during His earthly ministry. As priests, we must also do the same.

My book, which I mentioned before, *Recover Your Blessing Birthright: Transforming Lives and Culture with the Gift of Words,* is a training resource for becoming an ambassador of the spoken blessing.

The revelation that our Kingdom assignment preceded us is liberating and inspiring. Our responsibility is to discover what's already in us, develop the potential, and release it to build God's Kingdom and the lives of others. The discovery process is different for everyone. The chapter on the Roadmap to Your Royal Identity will provide more insights.

The language of Hebrews 13: 20-21 TPT is a fitting blessing for me to release over you as empowerment for the fulfillment of your Kingdom assignment. "Now the God who brought us peace…make you perfect in every good work to do his will, working in you that which is wellpleasing in his sight, through Jesus Christ; to whom be glory for ever and ever. Amen."

Reflection and Action

What insights did you gain from this chapter?

_____

_____

_____

_____

Specify at least two actions you'll take based on the insights gained.

1. _____

_____

2. _____

_____

CHAPTER 19

BECOMING WHO YOU ALREADY ARE

For he knew all about us before we were born and he destined us from the beginning to share the likeness of his Son. This means the Son is the oldest among a vast family of brothers and sisters who will become just like him.

— *Romans 8:29 TPT*

Words from a scene in the original Lion King Walt Disney movie are forever etched in my mind. It's the scene where Mufasa scolds Simba for going to the Wastelands. Simba was too immature to embrace his kingly identity and destiny. He was oblivious to what could have happened to him. So, like any wise father, Mufasa counsels Simba about his identity and to safeguard his legacy. Mufasa's words to Simba could very well have been spoken to any one of us: "You have not yet become all that you can be."

In our soul, we must become who we already are in our spirit. To come forth in our royal identity, we must allow the life, righteous DNA, and glory of God in our new-born spirit to flow from the inside out, bringing us more and more into conformity with the image of Christ. From God's point of view, the process is already complete in Christ. He sees the end at the beginning, and the blood of Jesus has presented us perfect in Christ.[77] That's the supernatural dimension. In the natural, it's a lifelong process because of the involvement of our free will, and layers of memories stored in our subconscious. The word "becoming" captures the ongoing nature of the process. It indicates the present continuous tense (something happening now and continuing in the future). Still, there is hope in God's promise of Philippians 1:6, "Being confident of this, that he who began a good work in you will carry it on to completion until the day of Christ Jesus."

Lessons From the Caterpillar

The metamorphosis of a caterpillar into a butterfly is an excellent metaphor that helps us understand our becoming process. Metamorphosis originates from the Greek *metamorphoō*, meaning to change inwardly, transform, or **transfigure**.[78] Biologically, the process produces a complete and fundamental change in nature, function, form, structure, and appearance. The change involves developmental stages, where the old form is broken down and reconstructed into something entirely new. Spiritually, coming forth in our royal identity also involves a metamorphosis. We undergo fundamental change and are transformed into Christ's image and likeness.

These verses vividly convey the comprehensive change we must undergo as we transform from within.

> Do not conform to the pattern of this world but be transformed by the renewing of your mind. Then you will be able to test and approve what God's will is—his good, pleasing and perfect will. (Romans 12:2)
>
> And we all, who with unveiled faces contemplate the Lord's glory, are being transformed into his image with ever-increasing glory, which comes from the Lord, who is the Spirit. (2 Corinthians 3:18)

Like the caterpillar, whose outward appearance and nature change through a gradual but complete process, we're to be continually renewed in our thinking, behavior, and character by the Holy Spirit.

Let's gain some insights from the caterpillar's experience. The metamorphosis begins as the caterpillar enters the chrysalis stage. It forms a cocoon around itself for a period of outward stillness but profound internal transformation. During this time, the caterpillar undergoes a complete restructuring, as its old body breaks down and is replaced with entirely new structures, forming the butterfly. It's noteworthy that even while the earthbound caterpillar crawled around, it had the life force (potential) within its body for its glorious transformation. This life force initiates the chrysalis stage, forms the cocoon, and sustains the entire transformation process until the butterfly emerges.

Ephesians 4:22-24 describes our putting off and putting on: "You were taught, with regard to your former way of life, to put off your old self, which is being corrupted by its deceitful desires; to be made new in the attitude of your minds; and to put on the new self, created to be like God in true righteousness and holiness."

Colossians 3:9-10 mentions a similar process of laying aside the old self for the new: "Do not lie to each other, since you have taken off your old self with its practices and have put on the new self, which is being renewed in knowledge in the image of its Creator."

There is an important lesson in the caterpillar's stillness during the chrysalis phase of its transformation. It's the lesson of trusting, waiting, and yielding self-control. There's a significant paradox here. Our fallen soul (the target of the transformation process) likes to be in control and will not yield control until it has been transformed or renewed. What does this mean? We must be strengthened with the might of God in our spirit and, from our spirit, draw on the grace of God for His Spirit to do in us what we cannot do for ourselves. Philippians 2:13 gives us hope: "For it is God who works in you to will and to act in order to fulfill his good purpose."

Unlike the stillness of the chrysalis stage, the final phase before the butterfly emerges from its cocoon is marked by significant struggle. One of the most fascinating things I've discovered is that the struggles and seeming suffering that the butterfly experiences are purposeful. A well-intentioned, compassionate observer once tried to help a struggling butterfly by clipping its cocoon. The struggling butterfly was freed all right but instantly fell to the ground, unable to fly. Little did this "helper" know that the struggle was essential to the process. By gradually pushing its way through its cocoon, the fluid in the butterfly's wings is forced into its thorax, making the wings light and flight-ready.

The parallel with the struggles and sufferings we often experience on our transformation journey is striking. We do not like discomfort, so we'll do anything to avoid whatever causes us to struggle or suffer. Our well-meaning friends and loved ones may even come to our rescue. But as it is for the butterfly, adversities serve a purpose. They're working for our benefit.

> I consider that our present sufferings are not worth comparing with the glory that will be revealed in us. (Romans 8:18)
>
> For our light affliction, which is but for a moment, is working for us a far more exceeding and eternal weight of glory, while we do not look at the things which are seen, but at the things which are not seen. For the things which are seen are temporary, but the things which are not seen are eternal. (2 Corinthians 4: 17-18 NKJV)

The key is to look beyond ourselves and keep our eyes fixed on the joy set before us—our lost glory restored and the image of Christ revealed in us.

Five Essentials for Transformation

Just as an earthbound caterpillar carries within itself the blueprint to become a glorious monarch, we also carry within our regenerated spirit everything we need to transform our soul. Second Peter 1:3-4 declares: "As His divine power has given to us all things that pertain to life and godliness, through the knowledge of Him who called us by glory and virtue, by which have been given to us exceedingly great and precious promises, that through these you may be partakers of the divine nature, having escaped the corruption that is in the world through lust."

Through its transformation process, a caterpillar comes forth as a glorious monarch. By partaking of God's divine nature, we're also coming forth in our royal identity into a life that glorifies God and displays His glory to the world. Our cooperation with the process is essential, so we'll look at five essentials that will enhance the process: Receiving the heavenly Father's love, renewing our minds, purging the subconscious, coming to the royal table, and going to the mount of transfiguration.

Receiving the Heavenly Father's Love

Many believers have come to faith in Jesus for years but still don't have a vital relationship with God as their heavenly Father. There may be different contributing factors. For some, the barrier may be a missing or unhealthy relationship with their biological father. I'm mindful of these situations and encourage you to seek help to heal such unresolved issues. You don't want anything to keep you from receiving the heavenly Father's loving embrace. He loves you perfectly, and His love will fill every love deficit in your life.

For many, however, the barrier to receiving the Father's love and embrace is a lack of revelation and understanding of their salvation experience. Although they've received Jesus, they haven't met the Father. I have a friend who was so in love with Jesus for having saved her from destruction that she couldn't stop lavishing her love on Him. One day, she experienced Jesus extending His hands to her and saying, "Come, let me take you to the Father." She met the Father that day, and He baptized her in His love, which has been the bedrock of her life ever since (for over fifty years).

The magnitude of Jesus' sacrificial death on our behalf is worthy of our eternal gratitude. Still, we need to be aware that the ultimate purpose of Jesus' redemptive mission was to reconnect us in our relationship with God. (Contrary to what many believe, the main purpose of Jesus' redemptive mission was not to save us from hell). Everything Jesus did was towards the end of our reconnection with the Father. His blood atoned for our sins and removed all enmity so we could again connect with the Father's holiness. His compassionate miracles of mercy and His teachings revealed what the Father was like.[79]

In John 14, we find Jesus telling His disciples that He's going away but would return for them so they could be with Him. Thomas was bold enough to speak up and admit they didn't know where He was going or how to get there. Jesus' response in John 14:6 is well-known: "I am the way and the truth and the life. No one comes to the Father except through me." Jesus then told the disciples that seeing Him was the same as seeing the Father.

Phillip needed something more. His request gave voice to the primary need of our hearts: "Lord, show us the Father and that will be enough for us." The language of the New Living Translation hits the heart of the matter: "Lord, show us the Father, and we will be satisfied." Jesus always intended the Father to be our destination. However, without the revelation, we can be stuck in the Way or at the Door. Jesus (the Way and the Door) wants us to meet the Father to encounter His loving embrace.

In reconnecting us to the Father, Jesus didn't stop with the work He accomplished through the cross. He became the Spirit of Sonship who constantly cries out to the heart of the Father from within us.

> Because you are his sons, God sent the Spirit of his Son into our hearts, the Spirit who calls out, "Abba, Father." (Galatians 4:6)

> And you did not receive the "spirit of religious duty," leading you back into the fear of never being good enough. But you have received the "Spirit of full acceptance," enfolding you into the family of God. And you will never feel orphaned, for as he rises up within us, our spirits join him in saying the words of tender affection, "Beloved Father!" For the Holy Spirit makes God's fatherhood real to us as he whispers into our innermost being, "You are God's beloved child!" (Romans 8:15-16 TPT)

Why is receiving the Father's love so essential to our becoming? Father's love is the reason for our existence and the bedrock of our royal identity as sons. We're made in the image of the Firstborn Royal Son, who is one with the Father, and we're being conformed to His image and likeness. The interruption of our relationship with God didn't only separate us from Him. It made us spiritual orphans, and Satan (the father of lies) stepped in to fill the void.

Embracing Father's love frees us from an orphan spirit and all its associated brokenness (including a hardened heart with limited relational capacity, rebellion, insecurity, self-reliance, approval seeking, self-rejection, competition, rivalry, and much more).

With the Father's love poured into our hearts by the Holy Spirit, as Romans 5:5 tells us, our capacity for healthy relationships is restored. Our hearts can beat again with love for God, others, and ourselves. We've said before that relationship is currency. It's one of the secrets to coming forth in our royal identity. Relationships with others are vital to fulfilling our destiny as royal sons and kings. We need different kinds of relationships for the various seasons of our becoming.

Renewing Our Minds with the Word of God

The mind is the thinking and decision-making faculty of our soul. With its divine order of being led by the spirit disrupted in the Fall, the mind became defiled by the DNA of the Tree of Knowledge. In its unrenewed state, the mind aligns with the flesh (sinful nature) and can neither understand the things of God nor please God.

> The person without the Spirit does not accept the things that come from the Spirit of God but considers them foolishness, and cannot understand them because they are discerned only through the Spirit. (1 Corinthians 2:14)

> Because the carnal mind is enmity against God; for it is not subject to the law of God, nor indeed can be. So then, those who are in the flesh cannot please God. (Romans 8:7-8 NKJV)

> So I tell you this, and insist on it in the Lord, that you must no longer live as the Gentiles do, in the futility of their thinking. They are darkened in their understanding and separated from the life of God because of the ignorance that is in them due to the hardening of their hearts. (Ephesians 4:17-18)

Romans 12:2 is the key biblical admonition for renewing our minds: "And do not be conformed to this world, but be transformed by the renewing of your mind, that you may prove what is that good and acceptable and perfect will of God." (NKJV) Philippians 4:8 also supplies a potent prescription for the renewing of the mind. I call it *Power8Thinking*™ — Occupying our minds with whatever is true, noble, right, pure, lovely, admirable, excellent, and praiseworthy.

From what we know about the Word of God as creative power, it is the divine instrument that will transform, renew, and recalibrate our minds. Hebrews 4:12 reveals the power of the Word to separate and reveal: "For the word of God is living and powerful, and sharper than any two-edged sword, piercing even to the division of soul and spirit, and of joints and marrow, and is a discerner of the thoughts and intents of the heart." (NKJV) In Jeremiah 20:9, the Word of God is fire, while in Jeremiah 23:29, it is both a fire and a hammer.

You get the idea. As a two-edged sword, fire, and a hammer, the Word of God will cut, separate, burn, and break the power structures of the unregenerated mind that opposes God so it can again align with God's design of being under the control of the spirit. We have a part to play, and we must be intentional. We must hear from the Lord the Word He'd have us apply to specific areas of our lives. Meditate on the Word, speak it aloud, and pray in faith. As Isaiah 55:11 promises, this Word from the mouth of the Lord will accomplish what it is sent to do. With a Word from the Lord, you can release His anointing upon it to do what God had appointed the prophet Jeremiah to accomplish: uproot and tear down, destroy and overthrow, build up and plant.[80]

Be mindful and discerning that the operation of the Word in our lives isn't always pleasant. Its operation may feel like the butterfly struggling to leave the cocoon. In these times, may we all learn to let patience have its perfect work and trust God.

In this dimension of renewing the mind, I call you forward into your destiny as a restorer. According to Isaiah 58:12 NKJV: "Those from among you shall build the old waste places; you shall raise up the foundations of many generations; and you shall be called the Repairer of the Breach, The Restorer of Streets to Dwell In."

You are coming forth as a restorer for such a time as this!

Purging the Subconscious

Renewing the mind relates to both the conscious and subconscious. However, the subconscious needs special attention because it impacts our lives more than the conscious mind. We're also unaware of its content until it expresses itself. This part of the mind works with the brain to store information and determine our responses to old and new experiences.

The subconscious is often referred to as our belief center. The strength of this system is influenced by the intensity of the impact of an experience and how often we think, hear, or see something. This highly complex part of our being reflects our cumulative personal, generational, and cultural experiences. In the chapter on What's Holding You Back, you read about the root system of the Tree of Knowledge reshaping our DNA and *psuche* refusing to let us go. Whenever I think of the subconscious, I think of it as the place inside us from which *psuche* dominates our lives. This association between the subconscious and the Tree of Knowledge gives us a good perspective of the depth of transformation needed in the subconscious.

I had a firsthand practical experience with the website for my last book that revealed two things about the subconscious I wouldn't otherwise have known—first, the subconscious fiercely guards against new information. Second, we must take intentional steps and be diligent, disciplined, and consistent in realigning our subconscious with God's original intent. Character matters in our transformation.

The consultant working with me on the project had done a few updates. However, although she assured me the changes were made, I couldn't see them on my computer. Refreshing my browser and restarting my computer didn't help. Eventually, she figured out what was happening and told me I needed to empty my cache. I had no idea what she meant or how to get it done, so I asked her to walk me through the steps. She did, and voilà! There they were! Her explanation that my computer kept retrieving old information from its auxiliary memory (cache) was eye-opening. Once we cleared this data source, the computer successfully accessed the new information.

Whatever is stored in the subconscious is not necessarily true. However, what matters is that it's believed to be true. In the Scriptures, the wrong beliefs of our subconscious are called strongholds. Second Corinthians 10:3-6 is often quoted by Christians in the context of spiritual warfare against Satan's operations. However, for the transformation we need to come forth in our royal identity, we must examine these verses from the perspective of our subconscious minds. I'm being intentional in providing language that's unfamiliar to stimulate fresh insights:

> For although we live in the natural realm, we don't wage a military campaign employing human weapons, using manipulation to achieve our aims. Instead, our spiritual weapons are energized with divine power to effectively dismantle the **defenses** behind which people hide. We can demolish every **deceptive fantasy** that opposes God and break through every **arrogant attitude** that is raised up in defiance of the true knowledge of God. We capture, like prisoners of war, **every thought** and insist that it bow in obedience to the Anointed One. Since we are armed with such dynamic weaponry, we stand ready to punish any trace of rebellion, as soon as you choose complete obedience. (TPT, emphasis added)

We have many spiritual weapons at our disposal in dealing with defenses, deceptive fantasies, arrogant attitudes, and rebellious thoughts generated from the subconscious. However, none is as potent as the blood of the cross of Jesus. The blood of the cross of Jesus is the ultimate remedy for transforming our subconscious minds. Just as it resets our identity and destiny, it will reset our subconscious by purging out the auxiliary memory from which it makes its high-speed retrievals.

> How much more shall the blood of Christ, who through the eternal Spirit offered himself without spot to God, **purge your conscience** from dead works to serve the living God? (Hebrews 9:14 KJV, emphasis added)

I often take this "purge," especially when receiving the Holy Communion. As you'll now see, coming to the Royal Table is an excellent transformational opportunity.

Coming to the Royal Table

For double emphasis on the continuous present action that this transformation essential requires, let me add a couple of words: *Keep on coming to the Royal Table!*

Above all, we keep on coming to the Royal Table because it is a place of intimate fellowship (communion) with the Lord. The Royal Table is a place of cherishing the Lord's presence and supernaturally receiving from Him. Do you remember Max Lucado's fictional character, Lucia, from Chapter 7? The secret to Lucia not adopting the village people's distorted perceptions of her was visiting Eli, her maker, daily and sitting in His workshop with Him. Being in Eli's presence and listening to what he said made her so secure in her identity that the village people's dots and stars couldn't stick to her.

This modern-day parable invites us to experience the kind of daily communion with the Lord at His Royal Table that knits our hearts together and reinforces our royal identity. As our High Priest in the Order of Melchizedek, Jesus wants us to receive the heavenly bread and wine He serves, just as Abram did in his Old Testament encounter of Genesis 14:18.

The Lord Jesus has left us the Holy Communion as our most powerful spiritual inheritance on this side of eternity. He invites us to partake in remembrance of Him.[81] We remember His redemptive sacrifice for us, renew the new covenant He has made on our behalf, and receive a transmission of His empowerment available to us. The bread and the wine are the most powerful transformational elements available to us.

Second Samuel 9 is a chapter that, on the surface, doesn't appear to have any relation to the Holy Communion. It's the account of King David honoring his covenant with Jonathan by showing kindness to his son Mephibosheth, who was lame in his feet and living in a dry, barren place called Lodebar. In the early years of ministry, the Lord gave me a signature message from this story: "The King Has Sent For You."

I saw the parallels between Mephibosheth and us living below our royal identity. Although born a prince, having lost his royal status in childhood, Mephibosheth had adopted a "dead dog" identity. King David's disclosure to Mephibosheth of the plan to restore all he had lost didn't elicit the response one would expect. Mephibosheth's response in 2 Samuel 9:8 reveals the depth of his distortion: "Mephibosheth bowed down and said, "What is your servant, that you should notice a dead dog like me?" However, King David had the ultimate cure for Mephibosheth's distorted fig leaf identity. The most striking detail about his restoration plan was King David's proclamation that Mephibosheth would eat bread at his table as one of his sons. King David made this proclamation four times in thirteen verses. And in three instances, he included the word "always." Mephibosheth had a permanent seat at the Royal Table as a son, and so do we!

What happens when we keep on eating bread at the Royal Table? Adam and Eve's eating of the Tree of Knowledge had caused its DNA to be implanted in our souls (more precisely, our subconscious). Jesus is the Tree of Life, and at His Royal Table, we have the privilege of eating the Tree of Life and reattaching ourselves to it. Receiving the blood of Jesus is receiving the Life of the True Vine. In this Life is the overcoming, resurrection power of God we all need for our transformation. It's the purging elixir for the subconscious. The more we eat and drink, the more the life force of the Tree of Life, the righteous DNA of Jesus, becomes fuel for our inner transformation or metamorphosis.

You'll recall reading about the seven places where Jesus shed His blood. This quote from Ana Mendez-Ferrell highlights the effect that the blood from the crown of thorns has on our minds.

> This blood crowned him as King of kings and Lord of lords. It gave Him the victory over the devil's empire. He conquered the government of the earth. This gives us the position of kings and the ability to govern with Christ. This blood conquered strongholds in the spiritual world and in the mind of man. By drinking this blood, we conquer our thought life so we can have the mind of Christ. **We appropriate for ourselves the conscience of Christ**.
>
> Jesus the man believed everything that was written about Him. He knew that everything He was in His spirit had to invade His entire human nature until He became the Christ in His whole being. He trained His mind to be subject to His spirit in order for Him to see Himself as He really was. He was Christ, the son of God. **Likewise,**

> through fellowship with His blood, we allow the truth of who we are to penetrate our mind, until we literally become everything that is written about us.[82] (Emphasis added)

I want to appropriate the conscience of Christ (including His subconscious). Don't you?

There's great benefit in coming to the Royal Table in our corporate gatherings and observing the protocols in those settings. Still, we must remember that since we're spiritual sons functioning in the Melchizedek Priestly Order through Jesus Christ, we have an open invitation to come to the Royal Table daily.

Didn't your spirit soar as you received these fresh insights about the Holy Communion? You'll be soaring to an even higher dimension as we move into the last of our five essentials for transformation.

Going to the Mount of Transfiguration

I framed this transformation essential as "prayer" when I wrote about it many years ago in the original identity manuscript. However, with the revelation I've received since then, I realized it involves much more than prayer. So, I've called it Going to the Mount of Transfiguration because it's an invitation to ascend in prayer. We often quote Ephesians 2:6: "And God raised us up with Christ and seated us with him in the heavenly realms in Christ Jesus." The question is, to what extent are we engaging in prayer from this ascended place?

We're being invited here to accompany Peter, James, and John to the Mount of Transfiguration with Jesus. There are three main reasons why responding to this invitational call to the Mount of Transfiguration is particularly beneficial. First, Jesus is the Living Word and spiritual mirror through which we're transformed from one degree of glory to another. Second, we have been raised with Him in heavenly places[83] (symbolized by the mountain). Thirdly, as Jesus demonstrated, prayer is vital in sustaining our relationship with the Father.

Luke's account of Jesus' transfiguration on the mountain contains a hidden mystery. It's the secret to becoming who we already are. I saved the best for last.

> **As he prayed**, his face began to glow until a blinding glory

streamed from him. A radiant glory illuminated his entire body. His brightness became so intense that it made his clothing blinding white, as multiple flashes of lightning. (Luke 9:29 TPT, emphasis added)

This is a true glory explosion! Blinding glory, radiant glory, brightness, multiple flashes of lightning. Face, body, clothing; all set aglow. The language of this translation presents what I consider a full ultra HD resolution of Second Corinthians 3:18: "But we all, with unveiled face, beholding as in a mirror the glory of the Lord, are being transformed into the same image from glory to glory, just as by the Spirit of the Lord." (NKJV)

Interestingly, the Bible does not reveal what Jesus was praying about. I heard a pastor say that 99% of our prayers are petitions, and we need to pray different kinds of prayers. I've been asking the Holy Spirit to help us take our position in the spirit realm and teach us to pray the kind of prayer Jesus prayed on the Mount of Transfiguration. I pray that we'll all experience the glory invasion and explosion that this combination of praying together with Jesus (the Living Word), praying like Him, and praying from heavenly places sponsors. In the holy exchange of prayer like this, we'll find the transformation we seek to become more of who we already are.

The Apostolic Prayer

It is fitting that we end this chapter with the prayer of Ephesians 3:14-21. It reinforces that we need each other to experience unprecedented dimensions of the Father's glorious riches and love. It's experienced in community, together with all the saints.

For this reason I kneel before the Father, from whom every family in heaven and on earth derives its name. I pray that out of his glorious riches he may strengthen you with power through his Spirit in your inner being, so that Christ may dwell in your hearts through faith. And I pray that you, being rooted and established in love, may have power, together with all the Lord's holy people, to grasp how wide and long and high and deep is the love of Christ, and to know this love that surpasses knowledge – that you may be filled to the measure of all the fullness of God. Now to him who is able to do immeasurably more than all we ask or imagine, according to his power that is at work within us, to him be glory in the church and in Christ Jesus throughout all generations, for ever and ever! Amen.

Expect immeasurably more!

Reflection and Action

What insights did you gain from this chapter?

_____

_____

_____

_____

Specify at least two actions you'll take based on the insights gained.

1. _____

_____

2. _____

_____

CHAPTER 20

ROADMAP TO YOUR ROYAL IDENTITY

You're not just trying to get somewhere. You're destined for royalty, and not just any road will get you there. You'll need courage, discipline, commitment, self-control, and perseverance to take the road less traveled.

— Marva Tyndale

Our royal identity discovery process is ongoing, and there will always be more of ourselves to discover. God is infinite, and the revelation concerning Him is progressive. The discovery of our royal identity is also progressive. Having created us in His image and likeness, God placed unique dimensions of Himself in each of us. We need a lifetime to discover the divine dimensions we embody. Still, only when we see Jesus Christ (the image of the invisible God) face-to-face will we fully know Him and ourselves. As First Corinthians 13:12 says, "For now we see only a reflection as in a mirror; then we shall see face to face. Now I know in part; then I shall know fully, even as I am fully known."

While the entire book is a roadmap for leaving fig leaves behind and coming forth in your royal identity, this chapter provides a customized navigation path. It bridges the gap between where you are and where you desire to be. This personalized roadmap presents seven identity components: Source, Purpose, Design, Potential, Vision, Productivity, and Destiny. All seven are essential to the discovery and experience of your royal identity. Each identity component has an action principle and is unlocked by a key question. The action principle highlights what you'll need to do to experience the reality of the truth associated with the component. The key question invites you to a greater level of personal acknowledgment and application.

We'll explore each identity component as a Service Stop. The discoveries you make at the Service Stops are cumulative, building on each other to advance your royal identity journey. The components are also interrelated. A summary chart at the end of the chapter will explain the connections.

Let's begin our journey through each Service Stop.

SERVICE STOP 1: SOURCE

Action Principle: Know God as your Source.

Where did I come from?

Your Source is God, the originator of all things about your royal identity. You were born into a family through your parents, but your roots are in God, your Creator. Divine love is the motivating force for your existence. You were made by love and for love. Knowing where you came from helps you know where you're going. Reconnecting with Creator God as your Source and heavenly Father is the only starting point that ensures genuine fulfillment and satisfaction in your journey through life. Jesus makes this reconnection possible.

By praying this prayer from your heart, you can receive Jesus and restore your connection with God as your Source and heavenly Father: "*Heavenly Father, I accept Your unfailing love for me and Your free gift of salvation through Jesus Christ. I ask You to forgive my sins, and I now invite Jesus into my heart as my Savior and Lord.*"

Congratulations! If this is your first time praying this prayer, you've made the most important decision you'll ever make. You're now on your way to getting to know the person God created you to be. You'll receive spiritual support and grow in faith by being in community with other followers of Jesus.

Since God is your Source, here's what's true about you. Your inherent value is great because you originated in God, you belong to God's human family, and He delights in lavishing His perfect unfailing love on you.

SERVICE STOP 2: PURPOSE

Action Principle: Discover and pursue your purpose.

Why am I here?

Your purpose represents the intent of God, your Source. You can be sure you're here on Earth for a purpose because you originated in the Creator God, an Intelligent and Purposeful Designer. Before God created the Earth, He planned for you to be alive at this particular time to fulfill a unique purpose. That is why you exist. While Source is the foundation of who you are, purpose is at the heart or center of your royal identity discovery process. You cannot truly know who you are until you know why you exist.

You'll be greatly relieved knowing you don't have to create or invent your purpose. God preordained your purpose before your birth. While reconnecting with Creator God as your Source and heavenly Father is the beginning of your royal identity discovery process, nurturing your relationship with Him through faith in Jesus Christ is the key to unveiling your purpose.

Ponder these questions and journal your thoughts as they're clues to your purpose:

- What do I dream of becoming or doing someday?
- What have others told me that I do well?
- What do I feel passionate about seeing changed, fixed, or improved?
- What things am I good at and have the most success doing?
- What type of work would I enjoy if money were not an issue?
- What people groups do I have a passion to serve?

Strangely, your pain is also a clue to your purpose. You may also do an inventory of your talents, skills, and abilities for clues. Above all, prayerfully ask God to reveal His purpose to you. Whether or not you're already fulfilling your purpose, I invite you to pray this prayer to enhance your discovery and pursuit. *"Thank you, heavenly Father, for the wonderful purpose you had in mind when you created me. I ask for your light to shine on my path and reveal the many dimensions of my purpose I'm yet to discover and explore. Help me advance steadily toward your good plans for my life. Amen"*

SERVICE STOP 3: DESIGN

Action Principle: Embrace your unique design.

How am I fashioned?

Your design is governed by your Source and purpose. Not only did God preordain your purpose before your birth. He also carefully and intricately designed you for that purpose. The late Dr. Myles Munroe shared this insight, "Everything you naturally have and inherently are is necessary for you to fulfill your purpose. Your height, race, skin color, language, physical features, and intellectual capacity are all designed for your purpose."

You originated in God, who designed you to represent Him in a unique way, and that makes you special. Although others may have similar talents, gifts, and abilities, no other person is exactly like you because no other person is here for the same purpose. You're an original work of art. You're God's masterpiece. Your design as a spirit being is consistent with your being of the God-kind and part of God's earthly family. Do not make your physical characteristics the focus of your attention. Your spirit is the eternal part of your being and the place where the secrets to the royal you are hidden.

SERVICE STOP 4: POTENTIAL

Action Principle: Release your potential.

What is my ability?

Your potential is determined by your design to meet the demands of your purpose as intended by your Source. What you can become or do is an untapped treasure that God has deposited in you, waiting to be accessed, developed, and realized. Remembering there's more to you than you are at any given time is an essential truth to take with you on your royal identity journey. You've not yet become all that you can be.

The capacity and value of any product are based on the material from which it is made, by whom it is made, and where and how it is made. Designer and specialty products are sold at a premium for this reason. Since you're the masterpiece of Creator God and originated in Him, God is the only true measure of your potential. You have the God-kind of potential.

Don't measure your potential by what you or others think about you, not even by your physical limitations, circumstances, or experiences. You'll start understanding your potential as you set your heart to believe the truth about the Source from which you originated, embrace your God-given purpose, and celebrate the unique way God fashioned you to reflect Him. Being connected to the Source from which you originated is the key to accessing, developing, and releasing your potential because what is true of other species of creation is also true for you. As plants and seeds discover their latent power when planted in the soil, so will you when you stay connected to God, your Source and heavenly Father.

SERVICE STOP 5: VISION

Action Principle: Develop your vision.

How do I perceive myself?

Your spiritual vision enables you to see your potential. Vision sees what is in you before it becomes visible in the natural. Because you share God's Spirit essence and also live in a physical body, God has created you with the capacity for both spiritual and natural vision. While natural vision is sight, spiritual vision is insight. With spiritual vision, you can perceive, understand, and see through the eyes of faith as God sees. This kind of vision is a function of the spiritual heart, not the physical eyes. Your ability for perception and insight is the most important gift God has given you to fulfill your purpose.

What does faith see? With eyes of faith, you recognize who you are presently, but above all, you also see yourself becoming the person God created you to be. As your spiritual vision develops, you'll discover the purpose for which God created you. You'll also see what Ecclesiastes 3:11 calls the "piece of eternity" God planted in your heart. With vision, you see the potential for greatness within you, and you're guided into productive action to fulfill your purpose.

Developing your spiritual vision is important because your life will lack focus without it, causing you to drift along aimlessly day after day. Pray for the eyes of your heart to be flooded with divine light. You need divine revelation to see yourself as God does. On the practical side, writing the vision God reveals to you will make it clearer and advance you toward its fulfillment in God's appointed time.

SERVICE STOP 6: PRODUCTIVITY

Action Principle: Increase your productivity.

How am I releasing my potential?

Your productivity is guided and inspired by your vision. All you've discovered in the previous Service Stops has prepared you for this crucial stage of your royal identity journey. Productivity is like the delivery system of the process. It transitions you from the discovery phase of your journey into the expression and experience of who you really are. Productivity means you're purposefully releasing and displaying your unique glory, your greatness.

Productivity produces a release in the two key dimensions of becoming and doing. First, you're allowing the nature and character of Christ (the One in whose image you were created) to be formed and expressed through you. Second, you're actively engaged in carrying out the Kingdom assignments and responsibilities ordained by God to fulfill your unique purpose and achieve your destiny.

You must strike a healthy balance between these two dimensions. Being transformed daily into Christ's image is as critical as engaging daily in your purpose-driven activities. What matters to God is not quantity but quality. Productivity is not trying to do more in your own strength. It's surrendering to the Holy Spirit and allowing Him to work through you to accomplish God's intent.

Remember these key thoughts: Productivity means work, but not all work is productive. Busyness does not equal productivity, so you must focus on what aligns with the vision God has given you and your purpose. True productivity is a partnership with God, doing what He does in union with Him to accomplish His will on Earth.

SERVICE STOP 7: DESTINY

Action Principle: Fulfill your Destiny.

How am I accomplishing my unique purpose?

Congratulations, you've arrived at the final Service Stop. Destiny is the cumulative experience of knowing God as your Source, discovering and pursuing your purpose, embracing your design, releasing your potential, developing your spiritual vision, and increasing your productivity.

Although destiny conveys a sense of finality, from an identity perspective, fulfilling your destiny is not a once-for-all experience. The ongoing pursuit of your Kingdom assignment (purpose) to uniquely reflect and represent God on Earth is what fulfilling your destiny is about.

Destiny fulfillment has a spiritual and a temporal component that parallels the two key identity dimensions of becoming who God says you are and doing what God designed you to accomplish. The spiritual component is directly related to the Source from which you originated. Since you came out from God as a spirit being, fulfilling your destiny means living a spirit-driven life in divine union with Christ to reflect His image and likeness. It also means nurturing a relationship with God throughout your lifetime in preparation for being united with Him eternally. You're designed for the same journey that Jesus describes in John 16:28 — *"I came from the Father and entered the world; now I am leaving the world and going back to the Father."*

From a temporal perspective, fulfilling your destiny means representing God's Kingdom interests on Earth by fulfilling the unique purpose for which He created you. Again, Jesus is the Model to which you aspire. You want to be able to say, as He said in John 17:4 — *"[Father] I have brought you glory on earth by finishing the work you gave me to do."*

How the Seven Components Interrelate

Three basic principles govern the interconnections between the seven identity components. First, each component contains everything necessary for the discovery and experience of the next. Second, apart from Source, which is self-existent, each component carries the cumulative benefit and effect of each preceding component. Third, the work of God's Spirit in you propels you from one component to the next.

COMPONENTS	CONNECTIONS	EXPLANATION
SOURCE	PURPOSE, DESIGN, AND POTENTIAL	Source initiates and ordains your PURPOSE, which establishes the specifications of your DESIGN and the extent of your POTENTIAL.
PURPOSE	SOURCE, DESIGN, POTENTIAL, VISION, PRODUCTIVITY AND DESTINY	Purpose is chosen by the intent of your SOURCE, which becomes the blueprint for your DESIGN, the indicator of your POTENTIAL, the catalyst for VISION and PRODUCTIVITY, and the pathway to DESTINY.
DESIGN	SOURCE, PURPOSE, POTENTIAL, AND VISION	Design is the artistry and glory reflection of your SOURCE, which provides clues to your PURPOSE, predicts your POTENTIAL, and creates VISION.
POTENTIAL	SOURCE, PURPOSE, DESIGN, PRODUCTIVITY	Potential is the capacity invested in you from your SOURCE as the hidden provision to fulfill your PURPOSE, which reflects your DESIGN and must be released as fuel for your PRODUCTIVITY.
VISION	DESIGN, PURPOSE, PRODUCTIVITY, AND DESTINY	Vision is a spiritual expression of DESIGN, which reveals PURPOSE, inspires, guides, and constrains PRODUCTIVITY, and sees DESTINY completed from the beginning.
PRODUCTIVITY	PURPOSE, POTENTIAL, VISION, AND DESTINY	Productivity is the practical pursuit of PURPOSE, which maximizes your POTENTIAL to create what VISION sees and fulfills DESTINY.
DESTINY	SOURCE, PURPOSE, VISION, AND PRODUCTIVITY	Destiny fulfills the intent of SOURCE and PURPOSE, which is the physical manifestation of VISION and the reward of PRODUCTIVITY.

To further explore these seven Service Stops, I invite you to visit The Personal Identity Roadmap on the Real Identity Discovery Ministries website.[84]

Heaven's Identity Billboard

God speaks in many ways. Many years ago, in the early phase of my royal identity journey, I had the fascinating experience of God broadcasting an identity message on a billboard. Although not visible to the natural eye, the words were piercing, and I've treasured them. I'll share them with you, trusting they'll guide you on your journey into royalty the way they've guided me.

"The extent to which the nature and character of Christ are released in you and experienced through you is the extent to which you are experiencing your royal identity."

In closing, I'll echo James 1:22 because applying the principles you've learned throughout the book isn't optional. "Do not merely listen to the word, and so deceive yourselves. Do what it says. Anyone who listens to the word but does not do what it says is like someone who looks at his face in a mirror and, after looking at himself, goes away and immediately forgets what he looks like. But whoever looks intently into the perfect law that gives freedom, and continues in it—not forgetting what they have heard, but doing it—they will be blessed in what they do."

Coming forth in your royal identity requires action, so let nothing hold you back!

One last Reflection and Action exercise, and then we'll launch into the acceptance and celebration of your royalty. Get ready to celebrate!

Reflection and Action

What insights did you gain from this chapter?

_____

_____

_____

_____

Specify at least two actions you'll take based on the insights gained.

1. _____

   _____

2. _____

   _____

CHAPTER 21

ACCEPT AND CELEBRATE YOUR ROYALTY

For the LORD your God is living among you.
He is a mighty savior.
He will take delight in you with gladness.
With his love, he will calm all your fears.
He will rejoice over you with joyful songs.

– Zephaniah 3:17 NLT

When we read the parable of the prodigal son from the father's perspective, we realize how much God, our heavenly Father, celebrates when we rediscover our royalty. You never want to forget this celebratory atmosphere of Luke 15:22-24. Not only that, you never want to miss the celebration, no matter what.

> But the father said to his servants, 'Quick! Bring the best robe and put it on him. Put a ring on his finger and sandals on his feet. Bring the fattened calf and kill it. Let's have a feast and celebrate. For this son of mine was dead and is alive again; he was lost and is found. So they began to celebrate.

On my 44th birthday, I had a life-changing experience. I gave myself permission to celebrate my royalty. There was no fanfare, just profound joy in celebrating who I was becoming. One simple action spoke volumes, broadcasted to the universe that I was coming forth in my royal identity.

I knew my family was planning a quiet dinner at home, but I couldn't ignore the strong inner urge to do something special for myself. Treating myself to a Baskin-Robbins ice cream cake felt just right. I popped into the neighborhood store on my way home from work. The perfect cake was waiting for me—Pralines 'n Cream.

It was a cold January evening, and I was perhaps the only one thinking of ice cream. The server was delighted to have a customer. She quickly took my order and reached for her pen and paper.

"What do you want me to write on the cake?"

"Happy Birthday to Me,' I said with exuberance.

Her hand froze. She looked up at me with eyes registering compassion and concern all at once. "You don't have anyone to buy you a birthday cake?"

"Me!" My hand crossed my chest in a gentle embrace. "I'm buying the cake for myself. It's my birthday today."

Silence overshadowed the rest of the transaction, snuffing out any congratulatory remarks that would otherwise have been offered. Still, I rejoiced as I left the store, cake in hand. Of course, when I arrived home, my children were as confused as the Baskin-Robbins server.

That day, I "went home" in a new way. I went home to my royal identity with a bold, new-found permission to celebrate me.

It's now your homecoming! Today, it's my utmost joy to welcome you home to your royal identity and celebrate you as the royalty that you are. That's who God made you to be, and He rejoices to see you becoming who you really are.

Your Royalty Celebration

For this grand occasion, I have a royalty celebration collection of poetic expressions, blessings, prayers, and personal affirmations just for you.

- Celebrate the ReDiscovered Man and Woman.
- A Love Blessing from the Father's Heart to Yours.
- An Identity Prayer of Praise.
- Personal Royal Affirmations.

Celebrate the ReDiscovered Man and Woman

While our gender-neutral spirit essence is at the core of our royal identity, it does not diminish the glory of our binary creation design as male and female. Coming forth in your royal identity will require rediscovering the honor, value, and intrinsic worth of who you are and your unique role as a male or female. I've deeply treasured these poetic expressions that Andrea Boweya authored in her book *The Heart of a Good Thing: New Beginnings of Bold Love in Your Relationships and Marriage*.[85] I invite you to read and accept each of these poetic expressions.

I Am A Man of Honour

At my core, I am a man of great wisdom

A visionary, an ordained planter of seed

One destined to be a priest, even far beyond what the eyes can see

I am a hero, warrior, leader, lion, and yet a lamb

I am a man of honour.

I have an uncommon depth of wealth within

My potential for generational influence is yet deep

I am a destined forerunner in my unique lane

I am designed to leap beyond every mountain.

I have the blessing of new beginnings;

there is grace for every day to come.

The surpassing greatness of God's power is towards me

As a brother, uncle, nephew, father, husband, friend, and son

I am a hero, warrior, leader, lion, yet a lamb

I am a man of honour.

© Andrea Boweya, The Heart of a Good Thing.

I Am A Woman of Worth

I am enough

I am a great gift

I am worthy of esteem

A destined generational lifeline for many

Even when challenged at my core

I am a heart of strength, vulnerability, and profound capacity

I am a Woman of Worth.

I am beautiful in so many ways

I am unique in depth

resilience, and character

In all I face, I am the beloved of God

I am crowned with grace and honoured by my heavenly Father.

I am a true nurturer of souls, a creative life force,

a channel of favour

I am a heart of strength, vulnerability, and profound capacity

I am Enough

I am a great gift

I am the heart of a good thing

I am a Woman of Worth.

© Andrea Boweya, *The Heart of a Good Thing.*

A Love Blessing from the Father's Heart to Yours[86]

On behalf of the Heavenly Father, I speak this love blessing from His heart into your eternal spirit.

My beloved son, my beloved daughter, whether or not you have known the love of a biological father, I call you home to my perfect, unconditional love for you. Not the love that the world offers, but the love you have been seeking all your life.

I am your perfect Heavenly Father and the very source of your life. I knew you before you were conceived in your mother's womb. You are not orphaned or illegitimate. You are not a mistake, and you are not an accident. I purposefully chose you in love for myself.

I have always loved you with everlasting love, and nothing will ever cause me to love you any more or any less. Call me Father, Abba (Daddy), even now as I embrace you, my beloved child. I will never leave you or forsake you.

Today, I bless you to receive the sufficiency of my love for all your needs. Will you surrender every wrong belief about me and my love? Will you allow my perfect love to wipe away every tear, heal every pain, fill up what is missing, drive away every fear, and empower you for a prosperous, fulfilling journey through life?

I bless you to be rooted and grounded in my extravagant, unfailing love as the bedrock of your life. As of this day, in your relationship with me and with others, may you experience the many dimensions of my love, knowing that nothing can separate you from my love for you.

I bless and empower you to be a channel of my love wherever you go. As you have freely received my love, I bless you with the grace and courage you need to gladly give away my love to everyone, everywhere.

My blessing is now upon your life, and you are blessed indeed.

Do you receive this blessing? Now plant it deep in your heart with a sincere "Amen."

An Identity Prayer of Praise

Lord! I'm bursting with joy over what you've done for me! My lips are full of perpetual praise. I'm boasting of you and all your works. Join me, everyone! Let's praise the Lord together. Let's make him famous! Let's make his name glorious to all. (Psalm 34:1-3 TPT)

My soul magnifies the Lord, and my spirit rejoices in Christ, my Savior. (Luke 1:46)

You have bestowed grace and glory upon me, withholding no good thing from me. (Psalm 84:11)

You have given me a crown of beauty instead of ashes, the oil of joy instead of mourning, and a garment of praise instead of a spirit of despair. With the life force of your righteousness transforming my life, I have become an oak of righteousness, a planting of the Lord for the display of His glory. (Isaiah 61:3)

All who see me will acknowledge that I am a crown of glory in the hand of the Lord and a royal diadem in His hand. (Isaiah 62:3)

The Lord has done this, and it is marvelous in our eyes. (Psalm 118:23)

Heavenly Father, let my royalty be to the praise of your glory, forever and ever. Amen!

Personal Royal Affirmations

I am royalty!

In my royalty, I put God's glory on display.

I am priceless and original, made in the image and likeness of God, my heavenly Father and Creator.

I am not an imitation, counterfeit, or cheap copy.

My life is not a mishap, mistake, or accident.

God chose for me to be alive at this time. He has appointed me for such a time as this.

I am God's masterpiece, His treasured possession, and His beloved.

The Spirit of the Great and Mighty God lives in me.

There is greatness in me. My greatness is my glory.

I refuse to hide my glory behind a mask, fig leaf, or under a bushel.

I will arise. I will shine. My light has come.

This is my appointed time and season to fulfill my unique Kingdom assignment.

I refuse to disappoint God. I will not waste or squander the investment of His glory and righteousness in me.

I refuse to hinder God's purposes on Earth any longer.

I am free of every limitation.

I will leap and come forth like a calf released from a stall.

I have found the truth about who I am and will continue living in that truth.

I believe God will finish His good work in me to His honor and glory.

About the Author

Rev. Dr. Marva Tyndale is an ordained minister and the Founder-Director of Real Identity Discovery Ministries. Her core mission is spiritual advocacy (intercession) on behalf of the next generation, and empowering others to discover their royal identity to fulfill their God-assigned Kingdom purpose.

Marva has authored many strategic resources to advance her mission as a messenger of hope to the generations. Her award-winning book, *Ready. Set. Not Yet! Secrets for Teens about Sex* presents the creation perspective on human sexuality and practical strategies for pursuing sexual wholeness. *Ready. Set. Not Yet!* was one of the 2023 Word Award winners, a prestigious Canadian writing competition led by the Word Guild. Marva is passionate about coaching others to achieve their publication dreams and enhance their Kingdom and generational legacy.

Marva's mantle as an ambassador of the spoken blessing and her landmark resource, *Recover Your Blessing Birthright: Transforming Lives and Culture with the Gift of Words,* have an international impact and enrich many lives at all ages and stages. As a Kingdom Chaplain, she's also dedicated to seeing the chaplaincy horizons of spiritual care and cultural transformation enlarged. Marva is a dynamic speaker and Bible teacher who delivers life-transforming messages through the pulpit, conferences, seminars, and retreats.

Above all, Marva values her royal identity as the beloved daughter of her heavenly Father. She is a mother and grandmother and lives in Mississauga, Ontario, Canada, with her spouse, Maurice.

Please visit
realidteaching.org and
readysetnotyet.com
for more information.

ENDNOTES

1. Holy Bible, New Living Translation, Premium Gift and Award Edition. Commentary on the Book of Ephesians. (Wheaton: Tyndale House Publishers, Inc., 2003), 671.
2. See Mark 8:22-26.
3. https://www.biblestudytools.com/lexicons/greek/nas/doxa.html, accessed Dec.10, 2024.
4. See Genesis 3:22-24.
5. See Isaiah 14:12-14, Ezekiel 28:11-19.
6. See Genesis 3:7, 10.
7. See Genesis 3:17.
8. See Genesis 2:18.
9. See Proverbs 10:11, Matthew 12:34, Luke 6:45, Romans 10:8, 10,17.
10. See Hebrews 12:24.
11. https://www.poetryfoundation.org/poems/46951/humpty-dumpty-sat-on-a-wall, accessed Dec. 20, 2024.
12. See 2 Corinthians 5:17, 21.
13. https://www.youtube.com/shorts/muK4fs6Fq50.
14. Andrea Boweya, The Heart of a Good Thing: New Beginnings of Bold Love in Your Relationships and Marriage (Toronto, ON: Shidaanikei Publishers Incorporated, 2021). Second Edition, 27.
15. See Luke 19:10.
16. Boweya, 21.
17. See Genesis 3:16.
18. See Genesis 3:17-19.
19. See Romans 8:15-16.
20. See James 1:21, Romans 12:2.
21. Ana Mendez-Ferrell, Eat My Flesh, Drink My Blood: The greatest Inheritance of power and revelation that Jesus left us (Ponte Vedra, FL: Voice Of The Light Ministries, 2006), 84.
22. Arthur Burk, Relentless Generational Blessings (Anaheim, CA: Plumbline Ministries, 2008), 96.
23. See Genesis 4:3-8, 9:22-25, 25:28, 27:5-17, 37:1-36.
24. https://www.youtube.com/watch?v=il0zQRO6Xr4&list=PLbwvmfmZzC_APIJBEC19K7jAM9-Ygo0Pu
25. See John 3: 1-8.
26. See Luke 1:5-25, 57-80.
27. https://www.youtube.com/watch?v=b0UT__MVfhk&list=PLbwvmfmZzC_Asv05lp5BnONLGubl-QTcT.
28. Max Lucado, You Are Special (Wheaton: Crossway Books, 1997).
29. See Ephesians 3:17 Voice.
30. See Genesis 3:15.
31. See Matthew 12:22-24, Luke 11:14-16.
32. See John 10:20, 33.
33. See Numbers 14:34.
34. Judges 6:13a.
35. Judges 6:15.
36. John Powell, Why Am I Afraid to Tell You Who I Am? Insights into Personal Growth (Niles: Argus Communications, 1974), 26-40.
37. Dr. Rajan Thiagarajah, 31 Revelations about the Blood of Christ (Western Australia: Mighty Living Waters Life Fellowship, 2010), 110.
38. See Exodus 12:1-30.
39. See 1 Corinthians 5:7, Hebrews 9:12.
40. The information for this segment is gathered from two sources: Ana Mendez-Ferrell, Eat My Flesh, Drink My Blood: The Greatest Inheritance of Power and Revelation that Jesus left us (Ponte Vedra, FL: Voice Of The Light Ministries, 2006); Dr. Frances Myles, Dangerous Prayers from the Courts of Heaven that Destroy Evil Altars: Supernatural Keys for Silencing

Evil Altars Permanently (Shippensburg, Destiny Image Publishers, Inc. 2021).
41. See Exodus 19:6, Isaiah 61:6, 1 Peter 2:9, Revelation 1:6, 5:10, 20:6.
42. See John 6:53-57.
43. Andrew Murray, The Blood of The Cross (New Kensington, Whitaker House, 1981), 9.
44. See 1 Corinthians 15:45, John 15: 5, Revelation 2:7.
45. See Matthew 4:1-11.
46. Ana Mendez-Ferrell, 67.
47. See 1 John 1:9, Hebrews 8:12 NKJV, 1 Kings 18:30-39, Psalm 103:16, John 15, Colossians 1:20 TPT, Mark 11:14 NKJV, James 1:21, Philippians 2:13, Psalm 103:1, Psalm 34:3.
48. See Genesis 1:10, 12,18,20,25.
49. See John 5:30, 14:10, 12:49.
50. See Ephesians 2:6.
51. See 1 John 5:14-15.
52. See John 17:22-23, Ephesians 5:27.
53. See 1 Chronicles 28-29.
54. See 1 Timothy 6:15, Revelation 19:16.
55. See John 17:23.
56. See Luke 2:49 KJV.
57. See 1 Samuel 13:14, Acts 13:22.
58. See 1 Peter 2:9, Revelation 1:6, Revelation 5:10.
59. See Genesis 17:7.
60. See Luke 15:25-31 for the exchange between the father and the older son.
61. Bill and Beni Johnson, Morning and Evening in His Presence, Page 80.
62. See Genesis 26:24, Isaiah 20:3, 44:23, 45:8, Mark 10:45.
63. See Isaiah 43:10.
64. See Luke 2:49 NKJV.
65. See Ephesians 1:6 KJV.
66. Read Song of Songs 4:15-5:1 TPT for exquisite language about being the paradise Garden of the Lord Jesus, our Bridegroom-King.
67. See John 5:18, 10:30-33.
68. See Genesis 1:1, John 1:1-3.
69. See Mark 3:16-19, Matthew 10:1-4, Luke 6:12-16.
70. See Matthew 4:1-11.
71. See Isaiah 50:4-5, 1 Corinthians 2:9-13.
72. See celebratory poems in Chapter 21.
73. See Luke 5:36-39.
74. There are seven major spheres of culture that shape people's thinking: Religion, Family, Education, Government, Media, Arts and Entertainment, Business, and Health Care.
75. See Ed Silvoso, Ekklesia: Rediscovering God's Instrument for Global Transformation (Bloomington, MN: Chosen Books, 2014), 68,123-138.
76. Dudley Mayers with Marva Tyndale, Kingdom Chaplains Everywhere: Advancing Spiritual Care and Cultural Transformation (Toronto, ON: Shidaanikei, 2024).
77. See Isaiah 46:10, Hebrews 10:14.
78. Strong's Exhaustive Concordance, s.v. *"metamorphoō"* (3339).
79. See John 17:25-26.
80. See Jeremiah 1:10.
81. See 1 Corinthians 11:24-26.
82. Ana Mendez-Ferrell, 71-72.
83. See Ephesians 2:6.
84. https://realidteaching.org/personal-identity-roadmap/
85. Boweya, 104-105.
86. Mayers, 73-74.

www.ingramcontent.com/pod-product-compliance
Lightning Source LLC
Chambersburg PA
CBHW070545010526
44118CB00012B/1224